THE
POETIC TRADITION

*Essays on Greek, Latin,
and English Poetry*

The Percy Graeme Turnbull
Memorial Lectures on Poetry

*Delivered at The Johns Hopkins University
and published by The Johns Hopkins Press*

THE ENGLISH RENAISSANCE: FACT OR FICTION, by E. M. W. Tillyard
(1952)

THE POETRY OF GREEK TRAGEDY, by Richmond Lattimore (1958)

FOUR POETS ON POETRY, edited by Don Cameron Allen (1959)

THE MOMENT OF POETRY, edited by Don Cameron Allen (1962)

THE POETIC TRADITION: ESSAYS ON GREEK, LATIN, AND ENGLISH
POETRY, edited by Don Cameron Allen and Henry T. Rowell
(1968)

Don Cameron Allen and
Henry T. Rowell, Editors

THE POETIC TRADITION

Essays on Greek, Latin, and English Poetry

THE JOHNS HOPKINS PRESS
BALTIMORE

PREFACE

Since the beginning of written records, men have observed in the flow of human life both a similarity and a difference. Heraclitus of Ephesus, poet and philosopher, put this observation into the metaphor of a river which appeared to be the same but was always something else. Pleased by this figure, the fastidious Ovid phrased and rephrased it, making it part of the literary vocabulary of western culture. The temporal measurements of sunrise and sunset could be expressed in terms of a great torrent, always the same and yet ever new. "What was before is left behind, and what was not is, and all is momently new." The two parts of the comparison present the inevitable third: there is change in permanence, permanence in change. Other Romans were at home with this paradox, and, like Marcus Aurelius with his poignant awareness of being at the center of an immense alteration, employed it again and again. By the fourth century, the metaphor has the Christian authorization of Gregory the Greek and Augustine the Roman, but it is the last of the pagans, Claudian, who discovers, "far from the range of our minds, scarcely approached by the Gods," the great cavern of Time, where the river transformed into a serpent symbolizes the alteration of the permanent.

With the beginning of our own age, the constant river of change becomes a living philosophical pattern. For some men, like Alberti, it is an enigmatic vision of all existence, and it is so accepted by the new poets: Ronsard, DuBellay, Spenser, Shakespeare, Donne.

Wandering through the ruins of what once was the *caput mundi*, DuBellay, for example, saw in the Tiber itself the mighty lesson. All that was Rome is here; time destroys what seems firm, only change is permanent. By localizing the Ovidian figure, the author of *Les Regrets* makes the alteration which establishes the tradition. Tradition is always inescapable, but it is, as every artist knows, the innovator who refurnishes it with change, who makes it enduring. This very simple idea is still among us; and when he was near the end of his career, Yeats restated it as the problem of the poet in three well-known lines.

> Shakespearean fish swam the sea, far away from land;
> Romantic fish swam in nets coming to the hand;
> Who are all those fish that lie gasping on the strand?

The conviction that all great poets, Greek, Roman, English, and American, take what their ancestors have given them and change it, perhaps only slightly but enough to make it new, dominates the following seven essays; for all of these critics understand that poets do not dwell in a flat, dry land, but by the river of tradition and are sensitive to the permanence of its changes.

The following seven lectures were delivered during the academic year of 1965–66 at The Johns Hopkins University as the Percy Graeme Turnbull Memorial Lectures on Poetry. The editors wish to acknowledge, in the name of the university community, our gratitude to the Turnbull family of Baltimore for making this a regular feature of our intellectual life.

D. C. A.

H. T. R.

CONTENTS

THE
POETIC TRADITION

Essays on Greek, Latin,
and English Poetry

John H. Finley, Jr.

✤ PINDAR'S BEGINNINGS

Aristotle begins the Fifth Book of *The Metaphysics* with something like a sigh. Every branch of knowledge, he says, deals with causes and principles. But all these branches, he goes on, "mark off some entity or some class and concern themselves with that, not with being absolutely and *qua* being. They fail to give an account of being, but from it as point of departure—either identifying it to sense impression or assuming it by hypothesis—they with more or less rigor demonstrate the essentials of the genus that concerns them." Even Aristotle, it seems, knows the decline of wishing to lay hands on pure being, only to be deflected to some part of it—and, even then, not to the being of that part but to its structure. In spite of his respect for identity, he would no doubt be surprised to have his words applied to Pindar—indeed to anything in history—yet they come to mind because a first motive for studying great figures of the past is the wish to share their outlook and tone of feeling. But the desire to enter into a bygone mind and see the world with its eyes meets obstacles, raised partly by ourselves, partly by the incompleteness of the record, and the attempt to fill in lost details returns us to the secondary kinds of knowledge of which Aristotle complains. The greater the subject, the sharper is the falling away from the original hope to the actual gain, and study of Pindar is no exception. The central fact about him and the source of the exhilaration that he inspires is of course his sweeping and brilliant but at bottom natural and unstrained style. So far as a style may be shared, he shares it with Aeschylus, and it relates in some way to the great events of their lifetimes.

3

But whence he achieved it, what ideas were its precondition, and from what assumptions it took strength—all this is finally hidden in the state of being that eludes us. Hence the previous quotation from Aristotle. Let us trace some elements of this style in the hope of entering more fully into the mind that fused and united them.

Pindar owed much to two men of the generation just before his own, Theognis and Simonides. Douglas Young's recent edition of Theognis[1] imaginatively, at times ingeniously, presents the elegies as works of one man—a view that corroborates and advances that of E. Harrison's edition of 1902.[2] The conclusion is important; it makes a difference to be able to hear in the collection, not a Babel of voices, but a single voice, broken and interrupted, to be sure, by the tradition, but consistent in its tough self-trust and unblunted definiteness. From Homer through Sophocles we are used to learning of the hard instructions of time and suffering; not so in Theognis, who stays exactly who he is. Young sees in our collection,[3] first, fairly full remnants of an early group of poems reflecting Theognis' involvement at once with Cyrnus and with politics— which poems in pride of authorship and to avoid misquoting he deposited, Young thinks, under seal at the shrine of Apollo Prostaterius at Megara; then, much more fragmentary parts of two longer collections—one of which, says the Suda, extended to twenty-eight hundred verses—from later stages of his long and troubled life; finally, the present Second Book, the so-called Μοῦσα Παιδική (Poems to Boys), contemporaneous with the first group but kept separately. The Suda's notice suggests that all these groups, together with a poem on a Sicilian siege—perhaps, Harrison thinks,[4] that of Megara Hyblaea by Gelon in 483—survived in antiquity; but our tradition perpetuates an anthology, made by unknown hands on unknown principles, which seems to have reached Athens by the end of the fifth century. If the well-known poems near the start of the collection (39–68) on the rise of new classes in Megara are to be connected with the excesses which, according to Aristotle,[5] induced the return of the exiles, his travels

---

[1] *Theognis . . . . post Ernestum Diehl edidit Douglas Young* (Teubner, 1961).

[2] E. Harrison, *Studies in Theognis* (Cambridge, 1902).

[3] Young, *op. cit.*, pp. IX–XIV.

[4] Harrison, *op. cit.*, pp. 295–97.

[5] *Politics* 1300a 14–19, 1302b 25–32, 1304b 31–35. Harrison, *op. cit.*, pp. 301–3.

may date from that disturbed period; he says that he was in Sicily, Sparta, and Euboea (783–85), and the tradition that he was a citizen of Megara Hyblaea would fit those years. In another poem he speaks of spying, apparently from Attica, his own former fields, now tilled by strangers (825–30), and in Thebes he applies to himself, evidently through poverty, the name Aithon which the disguised Odysseus used in Ithaca; he also rebukes a servant girl as Odysseus did Melantho.[6] But he is in Megara when the Persians approach, as Herodotus describes their doing in the spring of 479 when Mardonius retired from the second occupation of Athens.[7] He addresses a Simonides and an Onomacritus, but it is uncertain whether they are the famous bearers of those names and, if so, whether he knew them in the Athens of their joint patron Hipparchus.[8] He inveighs against tyranny but is presumably thinking of the Megarian tyrant; at least, to judge by what seems his abuse of Miltiades and the Athenians for their attack in 506 on Chalcis and their spoliation of the rich proprietors of the Lelantine plain,[9] he is as hostile to the Athenian democracy. Socially and politically, he remains to the end the ἀγαθός (aristocrat) that he was born; in the clarity of his tastes and distastes, in his addiction to poetry, love, and wine, and in his unsinkable confidence he is the talented exemplar of a breed that neither learned nor forgot.

Much connects him with Pindar: parallels of theme and phrase between the elegies and the odes, the two men's overlapping years and the unlikelihood that they failed to meet, their common ties of firm cantonalism. But one reason outweighs the rest: namely, Pindar's quite different sense of his poetic function in the Epinicians and in the sacral poems, such as the Paeans and Parthenia. He personally speaks in the Epinicians, and his "I" and "we" mean Pindar;[10] in the sacral poems "I" and "we" tend to mean

---

[6] Vv. 1209–16. *Od.* XIX, 183; 71–88.

[7] Vv. 773–82. Herod. IX, 14.

[8] Vv. 469, 667, 1349, 503. For possible attribution of the poems to Simonides to a nearly contemporary Euenus or to the better known Euenus, the friend of Socrates, see C. M. Bowra, *Greek Lyric Poetry* (2nd ed.; Oxford, 1961), p. 385, n. 3.

[9] Vv. 891–94, with Young's note.

[10] Mary R. Lefkowitz, "Τῷ καὶ ἐγώ The First Person in Pindar," *H.S.C.P.* 67 (1963): 177–253. Mrs. Lefkowitz dispels such doubts that first persons in the Epinicians always mean Pindar, as those of H. Fränkel, *Dichtung und Philosophie des Frühen Griechentüms* (Philological Monographs, American Philological Assoc., XIII, 1951), p. 541, n. 1.

the chorus. The singer (or perhaps singers) of his Maiden-song[11] is less animated than Alcman's fresh and talkative girls, but she is as feminine. The Abderitan youths of the Second Paean and the Ceotes of the Fourth speak in the person of their cities: "I am a young city," say the former; "I am horseless and inexperienced in cattle-raising," say the latter.[12] This is the voice of the more ancient corporate tradition that descended to the choruses of tragedy; to please a god and woo his favor for a group or city was to speak in its name. Epic poets, by contrast, had sung as lone figures—it is for himself that Homer seeks inspiration in the first lines of the *Iliad* and the *Odyssey*—and this personal role of the singer, restrained in Homer, grew emphatic in Hesiod and the elegists. Their stance as teachers enhanced individuality; Hesiod is the earliest Greek whom we know well as a person; and the weight of self that thus attached to a singer seems with time to have infected the choral tradition. At least Alcman mentions himself,[13] though we do not know in what kind of poem; Ibycus at the Court of Polycrates turned choral toward monodic poetry; and in some fragments of the Paeans and Dithyrambs Pindar's "I" may mean himself.[14] The problem is complicated both by the fragmentary state of these poems and because, as Schadewaldt noted,[15] Pindar's "I" is often formal and bardic, not personal in any strict sense. It signifies his involvement in an occasion and usefully allows him emphasis and transition. This bardic "I" is quite different from

---

[11] Fr. 84 (Bowra). Cf. Alcman frs. 1, 9, 16, 19, 20, 23, 24, 32, 60 (Diehl).

[12] Frs. 36, 19; 38, 24.

[13] Fr. 94, less certainly 92, 93, 96. Bowra, *Greek Lyric Poetry*, p. 23, thinks the famous lines on the kingfisher and halcyons (fr. 94) from a prelude. If so, the poet may feel free to mention himself, in the manner of the Homeric Hymns, before the formal song begins.

[14] Several Paeans, including those in which the chorus refers to itself in the first person, contain usually near the start or end an "I" or "we" that probably means Pindar: near the end, *Pa.* 2, 65 (fr. 36); *Pa.* 5, 44 (fr. 39); *Pa.* 7b, 6 (fr. 42); *Pa.* 9, 21, 34–40; near the start, *Pa.* 6, 1–15, 58. So also the Dithyramb for the Athenians, fr. 63, 7–10. All these statements fit the chorus, but even if, as seems the case, they mean the poet, he evidently feels no ambiguity because he identifies himself with the chorus. As just noted, this genial license to choral poets to mention themselves (often to adduce inspiration or good intent) may go back as far as Alcman. Choral poets, though vocationally given to speaking in the person of the chorus, may have felt as entitled to self-statement as epic poets.

[15] "Der Aufbau des pindarischen Epinikion" (*Schriften der Königsberger Gelehrten Gesellschaft*, 5 [1928]: 3), 259–343.

the personal "I" characteristic of the monodic and elegiac poets and not uncharacteristic of Pindar in the Epinicians, and the difference returns us to his bond with Theognis. The Epinicians—also the Encomia, Scolia, and Dirges—were not communal or (except for the last) ancient choral forms; they look to men, not to gods, and breathe the new individualism of the sixth century; Simonides seems to have invented the Epinician as a more brilliant and laudatory replacement for the old victory chant, τήνελλα καλλίνικε (hail to the victor).[16] But, if so, Pindar as author of Epinicians—choral poems though they were—is not remote in function from Theognis as elegist. It is his place too to affirm, warn, attest to his powers, and assert his loyalties, hopes, and standards. His role as narrator is something else; that side of his art allies him with Simonides and we shall turn to it. But the brilliance of his choral language should not conceal the curiously hybrid mandate of the Epinician. As choral poem, it carried sacral and communal suggestions and through narrative opened toward gods and heroes; but as sung of a contemporary and in a festive setting, it fell heir also to legacies of the symposium and the elegy, and was intended not only to narrate but to affirm. In a part of his mind Pindar must have conceived himself as only a more resonant Theognis.

Echoes of language need not argue congeniality, and two men more different in native temperament would be hard to imagine: the one hard-minded, outright, invincibly himself, reflective but about actualities, uninterested in what he has not personally known, fierce in his loyalties and angered when they are crossed—the other eager to think well of the world, proud of his powers but pained rather than angered by misunderstanding and prompted by it to self-questioning, entranced by the remote scenes and figures of legend, a seeker of ultimates, inclined to look away from pain and struggle toward fulfillment and harmony. Of the Persian War Theognis characteristically singles out the bickering of the Greeks, Pindar, the flash of victory.[17] Yet their common ground tells something of Pindar. Harrison listed many verbal echoes in the odes,[18] and echoes of theme may be added. Pindar concludes

---

[16] See Bowra, *Greek Lyric Poetry*, pp. 310 f.

[17] Theognis, 780–81; Pindar, *I.* 5, 4–5, 48–50; *P.* 1, 75–78; frs. 64–66.

[18] *Op. cit.*, pp. 314–19.

the early *P.* 7 of 486 to the Alcmaeonid Megacles by regretting
the φθόνος (envy) that attends high achievements; then closes

φαντί γε μὰν
οὕτω κεν ἀνδρὶ παρμονίμαν
θάλλοισαν εὐδαιμονίαν
τὰ καὶ τὰ φέρεσθαι

"Indeed, they say, felicity that thus blooms steady for a man endures
this and that."

Similarly Theognis holds παρμόνιμον (permanent) only what is just
and god-given; he thinks ἀγαθός only the man who is able τά τε
καὶ τὰ φέρειν (to endure this and that) (197–98, 398). Harrison
shows Pindar repeating the latter phrase with further echoes of
Theognis, and plausibly says that φαντί (they say), in *P.* 7, 15,
seems to have him in mind. In the Theban ode *I.* 4, 33–35, composed not long after Plataea, Pindar sees the victor's family emerging after long misfortune into success—

ἔστιν δ' ἀφάνεια τύχας καὶ μαρναμένων
πρὶν τέλος ἄκρον ἱκέσθαι.
τῶν τε γὰρ καὶ τῶν διδοῖ

"There exists an inconspicuousness of luck even when men strive, until
they reach the steep end. She gives of this and that."

One must bear what the gods give, says Theognis, without exces-
sive dejection or joy, πρὶν τέλος ἄκρον ἰδεῖν (until one sees the steep
end) (594). Best not to hoard wealth but to use it for friends,
Pindar tells Chromius in *N.* 1, 31–32—

οὐκ ἔραμαι πολὺν ἐν μεγάρῳ πλοῦτον κατακρύψαις ἔχειν
ἀλλ' ἐόντων εὖ τε παθεῖν καὶ ἀκοῦσαι φίλοις ἐξαρκέων

"I love not to keep wealth hidden at home, but from what I have, to
live well and win a good name, supporting my friends."

Theognis has οὐκ ἔραμαι πλούτειν (I love not to be rich) (1155);
rather he wants only enough; let the bronze sky fall on him, he
elsewhere says,

εἰ μὴ ἐγὼ τοῖσιν μὲν ἐπαρκέσω οἵ με φιλεῦσιν (871)

"If I do not support those who love me."

These examples of verbal echoes may suffice; in addition are echoes of theme: for instance, the desirability of friendship with the ἀγαθοί,[19] honor toward them but deviousness—even the arts of the cuttlefish—toward the κακοί[20] (the base), the rare friend who shares danger,[21] the virtues of silence,[22] gold tested by the touchstone,[23] καιρός,[24] the impossibility of undoing the past,[25] shipwreck as metaphor for misfortune,[26] the poet's duty to share his σοφία[27] (wisdom), the rare union of looks and virtue,[28] the obligation to praise an enemy when he acts well,[29] the blame that attends even good men but the entire obscurity of common men.[30] A splendid quatrain of Theognis which, standing beside verses of the Persian era, seems to date from those years expresses a mood that Pindar shares in several late odes—[31]

> μήποτέ μοι μελέδημα νεώτερον ἄλλο φανείη
> ἀντ' ἀρετῆς σοφίης τ', ἀλλὰ τόδ' αἰὲν ἔχων
> τερποίμην φόρμιγγι καὶ ὀρχηθμῷ καὶ ἀοιδῇ
> καὶ μετὰ τῶν ἀγαθῶν ἐσθλὸν ἔχοιμι νόον (789–92).

"Let no other newer care be mine beyond worth and wisdom, but keeping these let me delight in lyre and dance and song and with the noble keep a worthy mind."

This feeling for poetry and friends expresses the two men's bond beneath all their differences: unspoiled taste for the old-fashioned code of their upbringing. In a changing age Theognis kept throughout his life this provincial clarity, with resulting shock but unwilted crispness. Pindar, no doubt by temperament but also through his early education in Athens and long ties with Delphi, looked more

[19] Theognis, 29–38, 69–72; Pindar, *P.* 10, 72; *P.* 2, 96.
[20] Theognis, 213–16, 1071–74; Pindar, *P.* 2, 83–84; *I.* 4, 51–52; fr. 235.
[21] Theognis, 103–4, 1163–64h; Pindar, *N.* 9, 37–38; *N.* 10, 78–79.
[22] Theognis, 359–60, 419–24; Pindar, *P.* 3, 83–84; *N.* 5, 16–18; *I.* 6, 72; fr. 234.
[23] Theognis, 417–18, 450, 499, 1105–6; Pindar, *P.* 10, 67–68; *N.* 4, 82.
[24] Theognis, 401; Pindar, *P.* 4, 286; *P.* 8, 7; *P.* 9, 78–79.
[25] Theognis, 583–84; Pindar, *O.* 2, 15–17.
[26] Theognis, 671–82, 856, 1202, 1361–62, 1375–76; Pindar, *O.* 12, 11–12; *P.* 11, 39–40; *I.* 6, 36–38.
[27] Theognis, 769–72, 1055–58; Pindar, *O.* 13, 49.
[28] Theognis, 933; Pindar, *N.* 3, 19; *I.* 7, 22.
[29] Theognis, 1079; Pindar, *P.* 9, 95–96.
[30] Theognis, 797–98; Pindar, *P.* 11, 29–30.
[31] Pindar, *N.* 8, 35–39; *P.* 11, 50–51; *I.* 7, 39–41; *P.* 8, 67–69.

hopefully on societies and cities other than his own and, as the
mighty events of his lifetime unfolded, he grew and opened with
them, yet without losing, as the last-quoted parallel makes clear,
his native standards. Few gains lack some loss, and the width of
Pindar's actual and imaginary worlds sometimes strained his old
ties.[32] Passionate addicts of athletics must have been surprised at
his Olympian blindness to the details of sport, and rigid ἀγαθοί
doubtless better liked and understood Theognis' edge and firm-
ness. Yet for all his sweep Pindar never lost touch with the lucid
teachings of his youth; their vehicle was the gnomic element of the
Epinician, and their most recent spokesman was Theognis.

On the surface, and perhaps in fact, Simonides was more important to Pindar. As inventor of the Epinician, he created both the
form of the song and the public expectation of it to which Pindar
in youth fell heir. If, as we saw, the early *P.* 7 of 486 glances to
Theognis, the first extant ode, *P.* 10 of 498, composed when he was
twenty, draws as clearly on Simonides. Happy and praiseworthy,
he says, is the man

> ὃς ἂν χερσὶν ἢ ποδῶν ἀρετᾷ κρατήσαις
> τὰ μέγιστ' ἀέθλων ἕλῃ τόλμᾳ τε καὶ σθένει (23–24).

"Who victorious in hand and merit of foot wins highest prizes by his
courage and strength."

This itemization of powers is in the spirit of Simonides' famous
ἐγκώμιον:

> ″Ανδρ' ἀγαθὸν μὲν ἀλαθέως γενέσθαι
> χαλεπὸν χερσίν τε καὶ ποσὶ καὶ νόῳ
> τετράγωνον ἄνευ ψόγου τετυγμένον (fr. 4. 1–3).

"It is hard to be truly a noble man, in hand and foot and mind fash-
ioned four-square, without reproach."

P. 10 was commissioned by the Thessalian dynast Thorax, later
notable for joining Hippias in urging Xerxes to his expedition;[33]
Simonides' Encomium was composed for the Thessalian Scopas,

---

[32] Pindar, *N.* 4, 36–43; *N.* 7.
[33] Herod., VII, 6, 130; IX, 1, 58.

and he wrote two other poems for the same family, one perhaps an Epinician, the other the celebrated dirge for the ruin of the clan under a collapsing dining hall.[34] It looks as if Pindar was launched on Epinicians through Simonides' *réclame* in Thessaly and the desire of the Aleuads to emulate the Scopads; even the myth of *P.* 10 treats in Perseus a hero who was venerated in Thessaly[35] and was the subject of a famous poem of Simonides (fr. 13), though whether or not he composed it for a Thessalian audience is unknown. In another early ode, *N.* 2, 10–12, Pindar's reference to the Pleiades matches the older poet's; for the latter Hermes Enagonius is the child of the most beautiful of the seven sisters (fr. 30); for Pindar, who prophesies his patron's mounting success, the rising Pleiades foretell Orion's coming. A number of other echoes connect them[36]—not few considering the scanty fragments of Simonides' choral poetry—and in *O.* 2, 96, the mysterious dual with which the noisy crows vainly chatter at the lordly eagle is taken by the scholiast to mean the uncle and nephew Simonides and Bacchylides. The three men met at Hieron's court as they must have done earlier, but in 476 Simonides was eighty and Pindar forty-two, and the period of formative influence was over.

But, as with Theognis, the formal sides of this influence far outweigh the verbal sides, and it is Pindar's creative adaptation of these—not by one step alone but continuously and mountingly—that shows his mind. The legends of the Mycenaean heroes, initially the province of epic ἀοιδοί, swept into choral poetry during the rise of the Greek city states and with it the flowering of their cults and celebrations. *Epici carminis onera lyra sustinentem,* says Quintilian of Stesichorus,[37] and the titles of his narrative odes—*Funeral Games of Pelias, Tale of Geryon, Boar Hunters, Eriphyle, Sack of Troy, Helen, Oresteia*—show him treating many cycles of legend. The sweeping scope of the Hesiodic Catalogue of Women, which traced through

---

[34] Cic. *de Or.*, II, 352; Quint. XI, 2, 14. Bowra, *Greek Lyric Poetry*, p. 326.

[35] L. R. Farnell, *The Cults of the Greek States*, IV, p. 104.

[36] On κενεαὶ ἐλπίδες fr. 5, 14; *N.* 8, 45. On the pains even of the demigods: fr. 7; *P.* 3, 86–87. On death as a wave awaiting rich and poor: frs. 8–9; *N.* 7, 17–20; 30–31. On Olympia as εὔδενδρον fr. 22; *O.* 8, 9. On silence: fr. 38; *N.* 5, 18. On being checked by the sea: fr. 28; *N.* 4, 36–37. On refined gold: fr. 50; *P.* 10, 67–68; *N.* 4, 82. μόνος ἅλιος ἐν οὐρανῷ fr. 52; *O.* 1, 5–6. On the impossibility of undoing something done: fr. 54; *O.* 2, 15–17. On appearance violating truth: fr. 55; *O.* 1, 28–29; *N.* 8, 34.

[37] XI, 1, 62.

their women the heroic lines of all parts of Greece, attests to the
contemporary taste for legends which Pausanias' description of the
throne at Amyclae and the so-called chest of Cypselus at Olympia
further illustrates.[38] Though he renounces a complete description
on the ground that the pictures were well known, he mentions
some forty scenes portrayed on the throne and virtually as many
in somewhat more detail on the chest. Few of all these are drawn
from Homer; they have far closer ties with the Hesiodic Catalogue,
and there is notable overlapping of subjects between Stesichorus
and the chest of Cypselus. In the generation just before Stesichorus
the dithyrambic choruses that, according to Herodotus,[39] Arion
taught at Corinth, each with a name—also Alcman's mythological
poems—show the same kind of interest. In this era of new pros-
perity and travel the Greek cities evidently took pleasure in each
other's legends, and if, being attached to local cult, choral poetry
expressed first of all a new pride of nationalism, the taste of the
times seems to have been as catholic as that of Athens in the period
of the tragic authors. It was this immense panorama of legend that
through invention of the Epinician Simonides opened to Pindar,
but with the new emphasis of a poetry directed to living men, not
to a god or cult. The intense revelations of monodic poets, the
signed vases of potters, the worthy or unworthy self-proclamations
of Theognis and Phocylides, the inquiries of Thales and Hecataeus,
the politics of Solon, Pittacus, and Cleisthenes, the sayings of wise
men, the pomp of tyrants, and the fame of athletes, all fit the
temper of Simonides' individualistic invention. But it is just in this
tone that Pindar differs from Simonides. Though employed by
individuals, he wanted to see himself as not merely a praiser of the
successful, much less as a lone and isolated voice, but in the earlier
manner as spokesman of communities. A guiding force of his development was his search for means of expressing this belief.

   Thin as are the choral fragments of Simonides, their contrast to
Pindar is striking. One Epinician fragment (23) humorously or
irreverently declares, as Pindar would never have done, that
Polydeuces or Heracles could not have opposed a young Euboean
boxer; another (22) puns on the name of the Aeginetan Κριός,
ram; two others (16, 17) seem to describe actual chariot races in

[38] III, 18, 6–16; V, 17–19.
[39] I, 23.

livelier detail than Pindar's; another (19), quoted to illustrate
Simonides' legendary avarice, euphemistically overpraises a mule
team. One catches or seems to catch the accent of a quick, amusing,
imaginative mind that takes athletics, if not at all in the sardonic
spirit of Xenophanes and Euripides yet lightly and informally.
Two fragments (20, 21) on the joy of success come nearer Pindar;
at least, the charming verses on the two weeks of windless calm in
winter when the halcyons breed express a Pindaric sense of peace
after struggle, though with characteristic Simonidean lightness.
His descriptions of the sea and birds carry the same fresh tone,
which in a quite contrasting mood fits the impressionable sorrow
of his famous dirges. Pindar does not yield to thoughts of life's
changes, swift as a dragon fly (6), or of mortal labor and worry
and death's terrible Charybdis (7–9). However genuine may be
thought his belief in the so-called Orphic doctrines of *O.* 2, they
extend to another life his bright affirmation of this life. A like contrast appears if one sets beside the limpidity and pathos of
Simonides' verses on the infant Perseus the radiance of Pindar's
on the birth of Iamus;[40] the one man by temperament saw the
quick interplay of lights and shades, the other a firmer brightness.
These differences culminate in Simonides' intellectuality; of Greek
poets he most nearly repeats Euripides' union of impressionability
with speculation. C. M. Bowra well illustrates from Theognis the
famous Encomium to Scopas,[41] surely the most tolerant of Greek
poems. If an ἀγαθός loses his good fortune, the gift of the gods,
Simonides asks, is he any longer ἀγαθός, and Theognis' troubled
life exemplifies the problem. Simonides characteristically expects
no stability in life but is content if a man is not spineless, knows
justice, and of his own will does nothing shameful (4. 19–29). He
is much more tentative than Theognis who, in all the changes that
he saw and underwent, never doubted that he was an ἀγαθός, hence
kept a toughness of conviction that is lacking in Simonides. By the
same token, Pindar, who surpasses Theognis in confident affirmation, stands far from Simonides' sympathetic but melancholy impressionability. The Persian Wars, to be sure, brought Simonides
in his poem for Leonidas and his celebrated inscriptions a tone

---

[40] Fr. 13. *O.* 6, 39–57.
[41] *Greek Lyric Poetry*, pp. 329–30.

seemingly of a new age—less individualistic, surer, more lapidary—
but it is a paradox that Pindar was then beyond the influence of
the man who influenced him most.

Thus his predecessors, if they tell much of his tradition, tell little
of his mind, except negatively and by contrast. Bacchylides' use
of clearly marked areas of either narrative or gnomic statement
shows at once his temperate nature and the two sides of the tradition, but Pindar's interweaving of these sides marks from the first
his bolder mood. Something unitary in his outlook evidently
guided him, and one way of following his development is to trace
this unifying principle as he grew more conscious of it.

Greek myth oscillated between the two poles of history and
exemplar—ἔργον (deed) and παράδειγμα (example)—and part of its
endless usability was that it rarely invoked the one without imply-
ing the other. If Homer first of all conceived himself as transmit-
ting bygone deeds in authentic detail, their illustrativeness as
showing the varieties of men and fates was also in his mind.
Odysseus saw the cities of many men and knew their minds; Hera
in the *Iliad* drops from Olympus as fast as darts the mind of a
much-traveled man who says in his shrewd heart, "Would I were
here or there."[42] To Homer, Odysseus and this unnamed traveler
had seen the panorama of the world, which comparison—for example, as between the Cyclopes and the Phaeacians—made still
more instructive. But the deep changes in Greek life from Homer's
time to Pindar's tended to force the issue between these two functions of mythology as past event and as prototype, and in the novel
present to tell the old stories simply for themselves breathed an
antiquarian spirit, like that, for instance, of Pherecydes of Leros.
By the same token to find relevance in the old stories was to be
more conscious of their force as exemplars—as if, though still
historical, they at the same time somehow transcended history in a
timeless exhibition of fates and characters. By temperament Pindar
intensely felt this commentary of the heroic on the present world;
it is the single deepest impulse of his thought and, being apparently
in his mind from the first, was to prove through resonance and
expansibility his means of echoing the great events of his time.
This sense of mighty exemplars is his bond with Aeschylus and the

[42] XV, 78–83.

Aeginetan pediments; conversely, it is what sets him apart from Theognis' crispness and Simonides' impressionability as child of a more spacious age.

Yet the early odes show him groping toward what was to become his conscious and characteristic mode of thought. In *P.* 10 of 498 writing, as we have seen, for a Thessalian celebration, he begins somewhat in the mode of Pherecydes—not through influence but simply from historical temper—by likening Thessaly to Lacedaemon because the line of Heracles rules in both. Then after saying, in Theognis' manner, that the victor's success shows both ancestry and, above all, a god's help and after the previously mentioned echo of Simonides in his list of the victor's powers and even a certain Simonidean sadness in the sense of their mortal limits, he suddenly breaks into the bright scene of Perseus among the Hyperboreans. "The Muse is never absent at their haunts. On all sides whirl dances of girls, the cry of lyres, and the ring of flutes. They wreathe their hair with golden laurel and feast in felicity. Disease and hated age touch not that holy breed, but clear of toil and war they dwell escaped from carping Nemesis" (37–44). In his circular mode of composition, already established in this early poem, Athene's guidance of Perseus harks back to the divine help that sped the victor, and the hero's arrival among the Hyperboreans fits the victor's at Delphi, but the tacit likeness of this blissful and magical people to the feasting Thessalians seems an effect of fancy rather than of plan. The Thessalians, he said earlier, possessed "no small share of the pleasant things of Hellas"—τῶν δ'ἐν Ἑλλάδι τερπνῶν λαχόντες οὐκ ὀλίγαν δόσιν (19–20). To his young imagination their northern opulence was nearly Hyperborean; Apollo's people had taken the one further step that released them from age and death. The myth contains Pindar's characteristic analogy of present to heroic actions, but the measure of his youth is not only or chiefly his evident admiration for his rich hosts—it is, rather, that the myth lacks any tone of conscious pronouncement, as if he felt the analogy but was not yet aware of its meaning for his art. Hence the charm and freshness of this ode, but also its relative lack of weight as compared to mature odes in which he illustrates by myth what he pronounces by aphorism. He evidently does not yet consciously see himself as one who judges the present by the past and shows their golden bonds of unity. He is so far chiefly an embellisher of the present, as is evident also from the somewhat hyperbolic *P.* 6 of 490 to the young Agrigentine magnate Thrasybulus, whose success at Delphi with his father's chariot—he apparently did not even drive it—Pindar likens to Antilochus' self-chosen death at Troy to save his father, Nestor. One seems to see in these poems something like Simonides' fancy, if not his lightness, and their moralisms recall Theognis. Though by intuition Pindar already looks to heroic prototypes, he as yet lacks a personally achieved scheme—a poetic stance between past and present—whereby he might make the arts of his predecessors his own.

Three powerful impulses toward self-knowledge—his own maturing, the drastic effect of the Persian War on a Theban, and his visit to Sicily three years after the war—brought his full powers into being. As for the first of these impulses, the opening of *N.* 5, a poem of the middle 480's, declares a new sense of his poetic function, which in turn is subtly illustrated in the myth. This is the first of a series of three odes to the sons of the Aeginetan Lampon, the last of which falls soon after Salamis; they were thus contemporaneous with the pediments of the Temple of Aphaea, which just preceded or spanned the war.[43] As if with reference to these, he begins by contrasting his ode to statues fixed on their bases; rather he says, let his song put out from Aegina on every merchantman and skiff proclaiming the victor and the new honor that he has brought the ancient line of Aeacus. In the following odes *I.* 6 and *I.* 5, he treats the two sacks of Troy which, as greatest feats of the Aeacids, were the subjects of the pediments now built or building, but the myth of *N.* 5, Peleus' marriage in distant Phthia to the sea nymph Thetis (22–37), touches him more closely through its bearing on himself as well as on the victor. If gods had innumerable unions with mortal women and thereby in their offspring brought something of their flash into the world, the opposite is very much rarer, and for a man to achieve a goddess was beyond mortal fortune. Pindar reverts twice again to Peleus' attainment of Thetis;[44] the thought of the serene gods at the wedding, seated on golden chairs, and of the singing of Apollo and the Muses conveyed to

[43] G. M. A. Richter, *Greek Art* (New York, 1959), p. 83; T. B. L. Webster, *J.H.S.* 55 (1931): 179–83.
[44] *P.* 3, 88–96; *N.* 4, 62–68.

him a perfection of happiness, like but greater than a victor's. Part of the import of the scene to him was clearly Apollo's lyre and the Muses' voices, and in this ode, just as Peleus journeyed overseas to win his immortal bride and the young pancratiast sailed abroad to his victory, so Pindar like an eagle sweeps across the sea and his ode lifts sail from Aegina (21, 51). Peleus' wedding is far more integral to the poem than was the Hyperborean banquet to *P.* 10; as crown and reward to the hero's virtues, it illuminates the Aeginetan glory now confirmed and adorned by the victor, and Pindar's ode, like Apollo's music, expresses the present, festal realization of justified joy.

Now, needless to say, the dating of fifth-century works is full of problems, and though Aeschylus' Danaid tetralogy is lately most often dated in the 460's by reason of the papyrus connecting it with a contest with Sophocles,[45] the question seems not quite settled. At least, the name Mesatos,[46] which appears in the papyrus, is known of a late fifth-century poet, hence raises the possibility that the Danaid production described by the papyrus was one of those revivals that are specifically attested of Aeschylus.[47] If the *Suppliants* is indeed one of his later plays, evidence should chiefly lie in idea, language, and metre, not in the papyrus. Even so, to accept provisionally a late date for the *Suppliants* is to see Pindar and not least the present ode *N.* 5 with new eyes. The reverberation that the age was to find in the legendary heroes is now clearly expressed and, among works that have come down to us, for the first time. Aeschylus in his huge theme of the transcendence of aboriginal crime and hatred in some form of final harmony was to apply the legendary stories to the present with unrivalled scope, but that was twenty years later. Pindar's judgment of the present by the same standard of legend—and not fancifully or through mere pleasure in the stories, as in his earliest, more Simonidean poems, but rather through achieved method and conscious intellectual stance—seems the authentic accent of a new age. To repeat, the identifying mark of this outlook is to conceive the legends neither as history, glorious but of another time, nor conversely as

---

[45] Printed in Murray's Oxford text (2nd ed.; 1955), 2.

[46] Scholium to Aristoph. *Wasps*, 1502; *Euripidis Epistolae* 5, 2, in R. Hercher, *Epistolographi Graeci* (Paris, 1871), p. 278, 11.

[47] The Laurentian *Vita* 12, in Murray's Oxford text, p. 371, 20–22.

only poignant or lively incidents, but as classic exemplars, fit to
clarify the actions of a society.

The two war odes *I.* 5 and *I.* 8, both composed for Aeginetans
respectively, in all likelihood soon after Salamis and after Plataea,[48]
convey with mounting command the maturing manner of *N.* 5.
As already mentioned, *I.* 5 is the last of the three odes to the sons
of Lampon; the second poem *I.* 6 had expressed the hope of a
crowning victory at Olympia, but if the younger son conceivably
tried and failed at Olympia in the late summer of 480, his failure
was caught up in the national triumph of two months later. This
is not the place to rehearse in detail either the arguments for the
date or the brilliance of the poem. The superb opening on the
primal goddess Theia, named by Hesiod as daughter of Gaia and
Ouranus and mother of the Sun, Moon, and Dawn, mystically
exalts a spirit of brightness felt in gold, ships, racing chariots, and
victory. Pindar's mood in these lines resembles that of the opening
of *O.* 1; in both passages gold conveys the glint of the heroic which,
shining in victory, gives it momentary tie with gods and heroes.
He goes on to explain his train of thought with exceptional clarity:
victors, he says, deserve ungrudging praise. "For among heroes too,
brave warriors achieved fame as their reward. They have been
celebrated with lyres and the full-toned cry of flutes a myriad time,
and worshipped for Zeus's sake have given theme to poets" (26–
29). The lines express the ascending scale from man to hero to god
that he later states at the start of *O.* 2, but its bearing on himself is
clearer here: a victor deserves praise because it has been accorded
the great heroes, who in turn have been the theme of poets Διὸς
ἕκατι (for the sake of Zeus). The achieved ground of his art could
hardly be more clearly stated: it is the example of the heroes who,
as seed of the gods, showed the working of divinity among men.
The several parts of Greece, he goes on in a passage second to
none in showing the bond between nationalism and hero-cult, have
their peculiar heroes, as has Aegina in the Aeacids (30–42). Then,
after praise of Achilles at Troy and of what he calls the tower of
virtues that has remained to Aegina, he rises to the famous lines on
Salamis: "And now Ajax's city, Salamis, could testify that it has

---

[48] C. M. Bowra, *Pindar* (Oxford, 1964), pp. 112, 407; J. H. Finley, Jr., "Pindar and
the Persian Invasion," *H.S.C.P.*, 63 (1958): 121–32.

been raised upright by sailors in Zeus's ruinous storm hailing with the death of countless men. Nevertheless quench boasting in silence; Zeus accords this and that, Zeus sovereign over all" (48–53). καὶ νῦν carries into the present the bravery and brilliance of the heroic past, but, as Farnell saw, the warning not to boast and the lines on Zeus's uncertain will—both most unusual statements, since Pindar did not think Aeginetans vainglorious—implies something yet to come. The Persians must still be in Greece and Plataea cannot yet have been fought; in sharing the great hour of his island patrons, Pindar had temporarily forgotten the plight of his native Thebes but returns to it in his reverent sense of waiting on Zeus. The bright gold that he sees in victory, the greatness of the heroes through their tie with the divine, the theme that thus descends to poets, and the recent proof that ancient greatness remains in Aegina—this lucid sequence of thought shows Pindar's achieved way of seeing both his times and himself.

The year between Salamis and Plataea must have been very hard for him—together with the years following Tanagra, the hardest period of his life. What Thucydides later called a δυναστεία ὀλίγων ἀνδρῶν (a junta of a few men)[49] drove the old Theban dislike for Athens into Medism, and Pindar's ties of training with Athens and of friendship with Aegina must have pulled against the love of home that he often expresses. The change of mood between *I*. 5 and *I*. 8 is the measure of his pain: while the former ode saw in Salamis the golden flash of victory, the latter sees after Plataea only the ruinousness of discord and the heavy price of its healing. Yet there is no profounder myth in the odes than that of *I*. 8 and its sonority shows him the master of his newly found medium. After the curious and touching oscillation of the opening as between his recent sorrow and new relief, he soon broaches his theme of reconciliation by invoking the legendary ties between the nymphs Thebe and Aegina, twin daughters of Asopus, and thence by familiar steps reaches the island nymph's union with Zeus and the birth of her child, the peerless Aeacus. But whereas the great deeds of the Aeacids formerly prompted only thoughts of glory, now Peleus' attainment of Thetis—the bright subject of *N*. 5—signifies error and loss. This is the myth that Aeschylus was to use in the *Pro-*

[49] III, 62, 3.

metheia—he evidently knew the ode and adapts a line from it:[50] how Zeus and Poseidon each passionately pursued Thetis, yet yielded to the warning of the ancient goddess Themis, a divinity of the Titanic generation preceding their own, that the sea nymph was destined to bear a son stronger than his father. She was there-fore given to the mortal Peleus, most honorable of men, and in Achilles bore him a still greater son, who saved the Greeks at Troy but died there. Though the Olympians were thus spared over-throw, it is as if discord and passion, even among them, carried an inevitable price of death and loss—the former in the brevity of Achilles' bright life, the latter in Thetis' sorrowful brush with evanescent mankind. Yet the ancient wisdom of Themis—she who, as mother of the Horae, is felt in the benign regularities of nature[51]—declared the deeper bond beneath the transient conflict, and the persistence of the gods testifies to the possibility of accord. Further, since nothing that the gods touch lacks brightness, Achilles' deeds at Troy, though touched also by mortal brevity, showed a saving power, and as in *I.* 5 Pindar declared the divine blood of the heroes to be the theme of poetry, so now he says that the Muses sang at Achilles' pyre and finds in that act the sanction of his lament for a kinsman of the victor (65–67). In *N.* 5 the singing of Apollo and the Muses at Peleus' wedding expressed the scene's relevance to himself as well as to the victor, but in these two later odes he ex-pounds his mandate more consciously and, in the present ode, with deepest feeling. He has fully fused the gnomic and narrative legacies of Theognis and Simonides into his own unity, and the depth of *I.* 8 shows not merely his pain in the year of Plataea but, what is more important, the scope with which he now sees his art. Myth has become for him a kind of other language with which to interpret the greater meaning of events, and his heroic analogues express also what is to his eyes the nobility of the task. If the classic is a mode of vision that endows transience with stability and wins firm forms out of passing incidents, these odes initiate the fifth-century classic.

The occasional nature of the odes—their endless involvement with new people and circumstances—creates, from the point of

---

[50] 37–38. *P.V.*, 922–23.
[51] Fr. 10, 6.

view of any rational discourse about them, both delight and despair. The iridescence of changing scenes causes them to swerve and vary much faster than epic and dramatic poems, with which they nevertheless share much in subject and outlook. As he says in *P.* 9, in one of his rare statements about his method: "Great deeds prompt many tellings, but choose and adorn short incidents from the mass, and the wise will hear. In all things, moreover, the moment is the summit" (76–79). That is to say, he knows that relatively to Homer and even to Stesichorus and other choral poets, he sets forth his heroic incidents tersely, yet he hopes that perceptive people will grasp their meaning, the more easily because relevance, καιρός, chiefly clarifies. The passage, and a few others to like effect,[52] show how carefully he has chosen his heroic incidents and, to his own mind, what illustrative weight they carry. His doctrine of καιρός expresses the unique relevance of the incident to the occasion and its aptness to his poem as embracing both the present and the archetypal past. The reason for citing these words is double: time prevents pursuing much further the anfractuosities of Pindar's ever-changing occasions, even in the Sicilian poems, yet this allusion to his method, composed in 474 just after his return from Sicily, breathes the majestic self-assurance of the odes for Hieron and Theron. To revert again briefly to his beginnings, his gnomic legacy from Theognis on the whole looks to occasions; elegies carried the mood of symposia, bright, immediate, and sententious. By contrast, Simonides' poems, though by reason of his temperament by no means without their sententious sides, as choral poems on the whole look to legend or at least drew on that tradition. By the time of his visit to Sicily in 476, Pindar, as we have seen, had strongly fused these two elements, but they remained recalcitrant, and it is not surprising that the Epinician as a form hardly survived Pindar's generation. For lack of any such stirring impulse as the Persian invasion, he might, one imagines, have relaxed his unifying grip to let his poems sink back again toward the mood of *P.* 10 and 6, bright enhancements of festive occasions. As it was, the novelty—and surely to some degree the shock—of alien Sicily forced him upon himself, and he supplied by coruscation what he lacked in familiarity. His position in Sicily suggests that of Plato

[52] *O.* 2, 83–86; *P.* 1, 81–82.

more than a century later. A reason for thinking Plato's Letters
genuine—particularly the Seventh and Eighth—is that they show
him, though he was older than Pindar and Dionysius II was
younger and unsteadier than Hieron and Theron, rallying in the
same way to assert the ideas that he brought with him. Coming at
the period when they did, *O*. 1 and 2 seem to express Pindar's
self-understanding as only novelty forces a man to do.

References in *O*. 1 and *N*. 1 to banquets and to his taking up
his lyre may mean, as Wilamowitz thought,[53] that he sang as a
lone voice at a dinner party, not through a chorus; *O*. 2 is a personal poem to Theron; only *O*. 3 reflects a traditional occasion like
those for which he composed in Greece. Moreover, in these new
cities he lacked the sense of local hero-cult of which he spoke feel-
ingly at Aegina in *I*. 5; hence he resorts to more general legends,
of Pelops and his cult at Olympia in *O*. 1, of Heracles' founding
of the games and planting of the Altis in *O*. 3, of the birth of
Heracles in *N*. 1. To clarify the import of these not obviously relevant stories forced him to explain his purpose, and the consolatory
O. 2 to the old and troubled Theron cast him further on his personal standards. The combined result of these outer and inner circumstances was a new pitch of self-declaration. Now for the first
time, and characteristically in later poems,[54] he sees himself as
spokesman of the Muses, who guide him to fuller knowledge and
confirm its truth. Though poetry, he says, can be dangerous and
deceptive, his own is therefore trustworthy; the sanction of his
mysterious power is that he has it through nature, not through
teaching.[55] Hesiod too had distinguished between true and false
poetry,[56] evidently because it was one thing to tell heroic stories in
traditional detail, another and harder thing to speak truth about
the gods and the origin of the world. Though, unlike Hesiod,
Pindar was concerned with legends, the changed Greece of his day
forced him, as we have seen, to present his myths not as history
but as exemplars, and everything depended on their illustrative
scope and traction. He clearly felt the mystery of his insight, which

---

[53] *O*. 1, 7; *N*. 1, 19–22. *Pindaros* (Berlin, 1922), p. 228.

[54] J. H. Finley, Jr., "The Date of *Paean* 6 and *Nemean* 7," *H.S.C.P.*, 60 (1951):
61–80, esp. 70–71.

[55] *O*. 1, 28–35; *O*. 2, 86–88.

[56] Theog. 27–28.

he could explain only as the Muses' gift. If the expression is traditional, his use of it is not. He too of course tells what he thinks actually once took place—hence his way of breaking off a story which, though true, strikes him as unworthy[57]—yet as the previously quoted passage on his method makes clear, he does not tell a story in detail and for itself, rather gives brilliant light to a single crowning incident, because of its illustrative meaning. Hence his purpose, if one may put it so, is more Hesiodic than Homeric; he wants to explain stable truths about the rewards and limits of life and about relationships to the heroes and gods. He is rather a revealer than a narrator, and it is astounding that the narrow base of athletic success should have prompted this visionary flight.

As suggested, formulations of recent odes now recur but with quasi-oracular tone. Thus the mystical brilliance that shone for him in *I.* 5 in the flash of gold, ships, chariots, and victory reappears in the gold, blazing like fire at night, at the start of *O.* 1. The water that just precedes it goes back to the short promissory *O.* 11, composed at Olympia before he left for Sicily; in that poem welcome rain resembles hymns of victory after the strain of effort. The next following lines of *O.* 1 on the stark sun in the empty sky elaborate the Homeric phrase χάλκεος οὐρανός (bronze sky), which in *P.* 10, 27 mortals cannot hope to climb. The sequence—water, gold like fire at night, and the sun in the empty sky—subtly relates to the music of victory, heroic greatness, and Zeus's unattainable transcendence, but the riddling character of the lines shows how deeply they reflect his private understanding. We also saw this mounting triad in a slightly different form in *I.* 5 and *I.* 8: victors are praised because the great heroes became the theme of poetry, themselves the seed of gods. He now almost formulaically states this sequence at the start of *O.* 2: "What man, what hero, what god shall we celebrate?" It is his previously achieved scheme that allows him this terseness. Yet sense of isolation also prompted more careful statement of his scheme than any hitherto; it is his subject in *O.* 1, and he expounds it in two ways, by adage or half by adage and by legend. As for the former, Pelops was not, as evil-minded people said, eaten by the gods; such impious stories are only a commentary

[57] *O.* 1, 35; *O.* 9, 35–39; *N.* 5, 14–18.

on those who tell them. On the contrary, the gods, far from being
cannibalistic, were only too generous to Pelops' father Tantalus, to
whom they offered immortality by sharing with him their nectar
and ambrosia (54–55). But in his mortal silliness he could not endure his bliss, and tried to share the gods' gifts with his human
boon companions; hence, together with his son Pelops, was expelled from Olympus. This initial contrast, which occupies roughly
the first half of the ode, constates an utter gulf between the gods
and men, not through the gods' desire but from men's vacuity,
which appears the greater through the evil and jealous stories to
which they are addicted. But Pelops on reaching maturity sought
at Olympia to win Hippodameia from her dangerous father
Oenomaus, who had already overtaken and killed thirteen suitors
in the chariot race that he set as marriage test. At the shore of the
gray sea Pelops prayed to Poseidon, who had loved him in his
youth on Olympus: "Great danger," he said, "attracts no supine
man. But since we must die, why should one sit in the shadow
futilely cosseting a nameless old age? I shall attempt this trial; only
give happy outcome" (81–85). Poseidon's magical apparition at
the hero's call and his gift to him of winged horses and a golden
chariot (87) attest both to the gods' faith and to the possibility of
heroism. The gold of Pelops' chariot restates the gold of the first
line, and Pelops' emergence into bright heroism from what would
otherwise have been the empty shadow of an unremembered life
shows the gold again shining out of darkness. Pelops thus illustrates
a position bridging the gulf between the serene gods and transient
mankind, and mortal life, though utterly distinct, as Pindar later
says in *N.* 6, from the divine permanence, yet keeps kinship with it.

There is no time to pursue through later odes either this basic
scheme or the poetic attitudes that subtly accompany it. The
alienness of his Sicilian visit, by forcing him to fix and declare the
ideas that he brought with him, affected him lastingly. He is henceforth more consciously the spokesman of the Muses, and the fervor
of his appeals to them shows that, whether he wished or not, he
now necessarily stood somewhat apart from any one place or setting, a revealer of the longer and the hidden, not merely an adorner
of the visible. Hence in part his future discomfort; for though he
doubtless returned with relief to his familiar world of the old Greek
cities, his scope got him misunderstanding at both Thebes and

Aegina.[58] This plight is as good a gauge as any of the distance that he had traveled from the clear world of Theognis' ἀγαθοί, and even from that of Simonides' color and impressionability. As was noted earlier, late odes from the years of the Athenian occupation of Boeotia and the ruin of his youthful world express unimpaired the code of fidelity to friends and singing which is his bond with Theognis, but the visionary endings of the latest odes, *P.* 8 and *N.* 11, show his gaze turned never more intently toward a farther light.

What then, more exactly, is the import of the scheme that he sets forth most clearly in *O.* 1 and that thus relates to poems before and after? The difficulty is that he does not, and surely cannot, say that the greatness of the semi-divine heroes is matched by any living man. As noted, Simonides' assertion that Polydeuces or Heracles could not have withstood the Euboean boxer whom he was praising would have been unthinkable to Pindar. Yet the heroes are relevant to the present, seemingly in two main ways: because, as human beings, not gods, they trusted their mortal courage and in so doing found divine support, and because knowledge of such actions, as the theme of poetry, reveals life's openness to strength and purpose and the just joy of their fulfillment. Occupying the middle ground between the changeless gods and transient mankind, the heroes are varyingly represented. Heracles after huge toil became, in the splendid line of *I.* 4, 66, χρυσέων οἴκων ἄναξ καὶ γαμβρὸς Ἥρας, "Lord of golden halls and Hera's son-in-law," and the Dioscuri live alternately on Olympus and beneath Therapne,[59] but Peleus and Cadmus later lost the perfect happiness of their weddings to goddesses,[60] and Ajax's fame was revived only after his death.[61] Similarly among mortals, the so-called Orphic doctrines of *O.* 2 and some fragments of the dirges[62] carry a just man's happiness to fulfilment in another life, but victory also catches momentarily a man's perfect joy. Men tacitly resemble the heroes in this gamut between lasting and momentary completeness, but music is on the side of permanence, and Pindar's pride in his function is

[58] *P.* 9, 79–96; *N.* 4, 36–43; *N.* 7.
[59] *P.* 11, 61–64; *N.* 10, 85–88.
[60] *P.* 3, 86–103.
[61] *I.* 4, 41–43; *N.* 7, 24–30; *N.* 8, 21–34.
[62] Frs. 114–17; 127; 131; 83, 8–11.

in his sense of lifting the transitory into the lasting. Unlike
Aeschylus, he is uninterested in evolution, and his figures ascend
not through historical steps, but through their own achievement
into vivid being. The short *I.* 3, which was later added to *I.* 4
after the victor's second success, gives unique comment on this way
of thought. It consists of a single triad of strophe, antistrophe, and
epode, and lacking time for a myth after his initial description of
the victor and his hard-pressed family, Pindar concludes simply:
"With rolling days life brings now this, now that. Unwounded yet
remain the demi-gods." Space forces him to a kind of ellipsis, and
as final commentary on this laborious clan he quite simply gives
the heroes. They are for him the exemplars, and the fifth-century
classic begins in his vision of them.

T. B. L. Webster

❧ EURIPIDES: TRADITIONALIST AND INNOVATOR

My title, "Euripides, traditionalist and innovator," is a reminder
rather than a program. It is a reminder first that the conditions
under which the ancient dramatist worked were very different
from the conditions under which the modern dramatist works and
allowed much less scope for innovation in scenery, costumes, production, language, and subject. It is a reminder secondly how little
we know, particularly how little we know about the detailed
chronology of Sophocles, who started producing thirteen years
before Euripides and survived him by a year, so that what seems
to us to be Euripidean innovation may in fact be traditional in the
sense that he borrowed it from an earlier play of Sophocles: we
cannot say, for instance, who invented the terrible spectacle of a
man coming onto the stage again after he has put out his eyes, or
had his eyes put out. Euripides' *Oedipus* is late, in his *Hecuba* the
blinding of Polymestor may be an innovation in the story, borrowed
either from his own earlier *Phoenix* or from Sophocles' *Oedipus;*
Euripides' *Phoenix* was certainly produced before 425 B.C. and
Sophocles' *Oedipus* may have been produced as early as 429. Probably Euripides' play was the earlier of the two, but, even so,
Sophocles may have used this type of spectacle earlier in another
play, or Aeschylus may have preceded them both.

Euripides produced all his tragedies, as far as we know, at the
city festival of Dionysos, which took place in March. Every year
three poets were chosen to produce three tragedies and one satyr
play each. They were chosen by the archon, the chief civil magis-
trate of Athens, who took office late in June. He also appointed to
each poet a choregos, who engaged, paid, and dressed the fifteen

27

members of the chorus and the flute-player, and the chief actor, who himself engaged his two assistant actors and any mutes that might be required. The poet provided script and music, and trained both actors and chorus. Euripides produced twenty-two times (i.e., eighty-eight plays) during the fifty years of his working life— on an average nearly every other year—but, in fact, his productions bunched considerably toward the end of his life, and his last five productions covered only seven years. Writing and producing at this rate he naturally used situations, scenes, and concatenations of scenes which had been successful before, whether in his own plays or the plays of others. For instance, scenes in which a girl or youth declares readiness to be killed as a sacrifice for family or country are good theater and show the unselfish heroism of the young: Euripides introduced them six times.[1]

Apart from the need to produce quickly, the conditions of production in Euripides' lifetime made for traditional drama. Scenery remained unchanged throughout the play: circular dancing floor or *orchestra* for the chorus, low stage with altar, central door flanked by panels of scenery representing either buildings (if the scene was a palace, temple, or camp) or rocks (if the scene was in the country). The roof above the door could be used, and a platform or *ekkyklema* could be rolled out of the central door to show a tableau. The crane or *mechane* could present a flying figure and land it on the stage. All these conventions (except perhaps the *mechane*) were established before Euripides began to produce. But sometimes a brilliant use may be called an innovation: Medea with the bodies of her children in her dragon-chariot above the palace while Jason and his attendants hammered vainly on the palace-doors below, or in the *Phoenissae* the shy Antigone led on to the roof of the palace by the old man so that he may point out over the heads of the audience the seven champions attacking Thebes.

Two uses of the *ekkyklema* seem startlingly new. In the *Cresphontes* Euripides wanted to show the awful moment when Merope is about to kill her sleeping son, but is stopped when she has already raised her axe by the old man, who recognizes him. "What a shudder this sent through the theater," says Plutarch, "in their fear that the old man would not stop her in time." This dramatic scene must

---

[1] *Heraclidae, Hecuba, Erechtheus, Phrixus B, Phoenissae, Iphigenia in Aulis.*

have been played on the *ekkyklema*, because nothing except the rolling platform could bring the sleeping boy before the eyes of the audience. In his *Andromeda* Sophocles had a scene in which Andromeda was chained to the rock (like Prometheus in Aeschylus' *Prometheus Vinctus*), but for his *Andromeda* thirty years later Euripides preferred to open the play with the *ekkyklema* rolling out with Andromeda already on the rock, so as to create at once the spectacle of the girl alone in the night, her laments only answered by a concealed Echo, waiting for the monster to come and devour her.

The limitation of actors to three automatically limited the number of speakers in any given scene to one, two, three, or four if the leader of the chorus is included. Any experiment with a larger number of speakers was therefore impossible. But mutes could be used not only for attendants, soldiers, and the like, but for characters: in the *Electra* Pylades is the silent shadow of Orestes all through the play; in the *Orestes* he has an important speaking part in two scenes but is silent in the last scene. This last scene of the *Orestes* shows Euripides at his most daring in the use of mutes and of the different levels in the Greek theater. The speakers are the leader of the excited chorus of women in the *orchestra*, Menelaos on the stage, Orestes on the roof, and Apollo above on the *mechane*. But the spectacle is increased by the mute servants of Menelaos, whom he tells to break in the door, by the mute Hermione, Elektra, and Pylades on the roof (Hermione has a knife held to her throat by Orestes; Elektra and Pylades brandish torches to set fire to the palace), and by the mute Helen, who is being taken to heaven by Apollo.

The metrical and musical shape of tragedy was also well established when Euripides began to write: actor-scenes in spoken iambics separated by odes in lyric meters sung by the chorus (and very occasionally by a subsidiary chorus) and sometimes by dialogues between actor and chorus in lyric or recitative or both. His plays show a steady development, which can be described in technical terms but is not so easy to interpret in terms of the impression which the poet wanted to create. (The following account is based on Zielinski for spoken iambics and A. M. Dale for other meters.)[2]

---

[2] Th. Zielinski, *Tragodoumenon* (Krakan, 1925); A. M. Dale, *Lyric Metres of Greek Drama* (Cambridge, 1948).

The spoken iambic trimeter of dialogue contains six naturally long syllables; it was permissible to resolve any of the first five of these into two short syllables. Aeschylus uses the permission once every nine lines in the *Persae* of 472 B.C., but only once every twenty lines in the *Oresteia* of 458 B.C. Euripides maintains roughly the same proportion as the *Oresteia*, down to the *Hippolytus* in 428 B.C.; from that time he steadily increases the proportion of resolved syllables so that in the plays of his last three years they average more than one every three lines. For the simple and unemotional phrase "children having been born" he uses at the beginning of the line παίδων γεγώτων in the *Medea* of 431 B.C., but nineteen years later in the *Ion* παῖδες γενόμενοι: the substitution can only be in the interests of rhythm. The actor of the late *Orestes* in 408 B.C. had to be prepared to follow the perfectly stable line 'Ορέστα, γαίας τῆσδ' ὑπερβαλόνθ' ὄρους with the very unstable line Παρράσιον οἰκεῖν δάπεδον ἐνιαυτοῦ κύκλον. In musical terms Euripides, as he progresses, introduces more and more variations on his basic iambic theme.

From 415 B.C. onward in all the surviving plays and four of the lost plays he has actor scenes in recitative trochaic tetrameters, the meter used by Tennyson in *Locksley Hall*. Here my title reminds me to ask "Traditionalist or Innovator"? The figures are interesting: Aeschylus *Persae* 472 B.C., two scenes amounting to 114 lines; none in any later play except the *Agamemnon* in 458 B.C., which has 29 lines; Sophocles, none until the *Oedipus Tyrannus*, which has 9 lines; 7 lines in the *Philoctetes* in 408 B.C.; 5 in the posthumous *Oedipus Coloneus*. For Euripides I give three examples, *Trojan Women*, 415 B.C., 16 lines; *Ion*, 412 B.C. three scenes amounting to 81 lines; *Iphigenia in Aulis*, three scenes amounting to 200 lines. In the *Persae* Aeschylus still liked the recitative trochaic scenes as a kind of middle level between spoken iambics and sung lyrics. But after that classical tragedy practically rejected them as blurring the contrast between spoken and sung, until Euripides revived them in 415 B.C. Once he had revived them, he developed them in the same way as iambics: in the *Persae* Aeschylus has only 16 resolved syllables in 114 lines; Euripides has 41 in the same number of lines in the *Orestes*. Clearly then in his late plays he wanted again to blur the contrast between spoken and sung, and within the trochaic scenes he also wanted the same sort of rhythmical variety that he had achieved in his late iambics.

When an actor uses recitative, and still more when he sings, he is moving out of his own sphere into the sphere of the chorus, to whom music belongs. Aeschylus and Sophocles normally reserved this transference for moments of great emotion (the only likely exception is the ball game in Sophocles' *Nausicaa*). The songs were divided, like choral odes, into metrically corresponding strophes and antistrophes; they were written in simple lyric meters or in recitative anapaests or dochmiacs. Euripides gradually abandoned all these restrictions. As early as 438 B.C. in the *Telephos* Agamemnon quarrels with Menelaos in recitative anapaests; in the prologue of the *Medea* in 431 B.C. Medeia sings of her distress in melic anapaests and the Nurse comments on her behavior in recitative anapaests. Neither of these scenes, nor the anapaestic vaporings of Phaidra early in the *Hippolytus* are moments of great emotion in the old sense; the contemporary Sophoclean Deianeira, who is at least as sorely tried as Medeia or Phaidra, never forsakes spoken iambics. In the plays after 428 B.C. melic anapaests and lyric meters become more common, but both monodies and lyric dialogues are still usually strophic. From 415 B.C. this patterning is often abandoned, and the actor sings freely in lyric meter as the poet chooses.

Many of these later songs would have been accepted even by conservative critics: for instance, the lamentations of Hekabe in the *Trojan Women* and the joyful recognition dialogue in the *Iphigenia in Tauris*—the evidence is their obvious influence on the three last plays of Sophocles. Perhaps even Ion's lovely *aubade*, as he sweeps the temple and drives away the birds, would have been accepted as a brilliant modernization of the ball-dance in Sophocles' *Nausicaa*.

But sometimes Euripides did things which must have made Sophocles shudder and Aeschylus turn in his grave. In the *Orestes* in 408 B.C. he does not use an ordinary iambic messenger speech to describe Orestes' attempt to kill Helen, but instead introduces a frightened Phrygian eunuch, who has escaped from the palace and sings 130 lines of free polymetric lyric divided into six sections by the spoken (or recitative?) iambic questions of the leader of the chorus. He tells of his escape, the miseries of Troy caused by Helen, the entry of Orestes and Pylades, their imprisonment of Helen's Phrygian slaves, their attack on Helen, the rally of the Phrygian slaves followed by the arrival of Hermione and the miraculous disappearance of Helen. This is a brilliant lyric narrative in the most modern musical style; we know that Euripides had comforted Timotheos, the Schönberg of his day, when his first concert failed, and we can justifiably see Timotheos' influence here. In fact a spoken iambic messenger speech, besides awaking too much sympathy with the victim, would have broken the elaborate sequence with which Euripides leads up to the final tableau of the play.

The sequence is worth considering for a moment. Orestes, Pylades, and Elektra have planned to murder Helen and to catch Hermione and use her as a hostage. Orestes and Pylades go in to do their work. Elektra sings an excited lyric dialogue with the chorus, who divide into halves to watch the two ways up to the central door. She goes on singing encouragement in extraordinary pizzicato lyric, as Helen cries out for help inside the house. Then the tone sinks to spoken iambics as Hermione enters and Elektra takes her into the trap. The chorus sing a strophe in dochmiacs rejoicing. Then the Phrygian comes out and sings his long description. This is followed by a brief dialogue in recitative trochaics as Orestes drives him in again. The whole interlude of the Phrygian is rounded off by the antistrophe of the chorus, who sing of the smoke already rising from the roof. The arrival of Menelaos and his order to break down the doors diverts the audience's attention while the tableau is set on the roof. When Orestes speaks again, he is on the roof with his sword at Hermione's throat, and Elektra and Pylades are brandishing torches. Sixty lines later Apollo appears with Helen on the *mechane*. Helen's disappearance had to be told, and the Phrygian's song is the only kind of narrative which fits into the crazy sequence culminating in Apollo's epiphany, which forces the mad mortals to return to sanity—or at any rate to the lines laid down by traditional legend.

This sequence suggests a major question and a minor question. The metrical and musical phenomena which we have been discussing clearly show that Euripides departs further and further from the texture of classical tragedy. The clear contrast between spoken and sung is weakened not only by introducing recitative for actor-dialogue and by giving actors the full range of choral lyric, even in situations which Aeschylus and Sophocles would have cast in spoken iambics, but also by the pizzicato, unstable character of late Euripidean spoken iambics themselves. Spoken and sung are no longer contrasted blocks: spoken itself has a new kind of volatile shimmer; it may give place to recitative, and recitative may fade into song. The major question to which we shall return is whether this change in texture corresponds to a change in Euripides' treatment of the story and the characters.

The minor question arises from the curious ambivalence of Greek lyric meter. Metrically long stretches of Ion's balletic *aubade* as he sweeps the temple are identical with Kreousa's later agonized account of her rape by Apollo. Whether they differed musically we have no means of telling. But Ion's *aubade* suggests that it would be wrong to interpret the Phrygian's polymetric song in the *Orestes* as an expression of his terror. It is rather a piece of musical and poetic phantasy which Euripides needs at this moment. Phantasy can be evoked by lyric meter and sophisticated music as well as agonized grief or exuberant joy. Phantasy is the best single word I can find to generalize the phrase that Gilbert Murray used to translate a line of a chorus in the *Hippolytus:* "The Apple-tree, the singing and the gold." The chorus there has just heard that Phaidra intends suicide, and they wish that they could escape from the horrors. In a lovely poetical lyric they wish that they could take refuge on the top of the mountains and there be changed into birds and fly to the West, where Phaethon's sisters weep for his death in tears of amber, or further still to the golden garden of the singing Hesperides. Earlier their opening song, when they come to inquire about Phaidra's health, begins: "A rock, they say, drips with the water of Ocean, hurling from its crags a flowing stream where pitchers may dip, where was a friend of mine, wetting scarlet cloths in river dew, and she cast them on the back of the warm and sunny rock. From her came the first news of the queen." This is washing day transposed into poetical and musical phantasy to contrast with Phaidra's prostration. Many other choral odes and a few monodies have this quality, and phantasy could be asserted as a world parallel to the world of cruel reality, a world into which the chorus could often and characters sometimes escape.

In every production the poet chose three "historical" legends for his three tragedies. Many of them had been dramatized before and were in this sense traditional, but the audience must have watched for the innovations in each new treatment. Euripides had two different methods of putting his three plays together. Before

415 B.C. he went for variety. In 415 B.C. and in four of the six later productions the three plays have some connection with each other. There is a little evidence that this change corresponded with a change in the order of production at the festival:[3] it is probable that from 450 B.C. to shortly after 420 B.C. each of the three competing poets produced one tragedy on each of the three days, but that after that each poet again produced all his three tragedies on the same day, and this gave the possibility of relating the tragedies to each other.

In 415 B.C. Euripides chose three chapters in the story of the Trojan War: in the first play the lost son of Priam and Hekabe is discovered in the young herdsman Paris, who defeats the sons of Priam in the games and narrowly escapes murder at the hands of Deiphobos. The second play is set in the Greek camp before Troy; Odysseus hoodwinks Agamemnon in compassing the death of the innocent Palamedes, whom he hates. The third play is the surviving *Trojan Women*, dealing with their sufferings after the capture of Troy. The impact of this play is immensely increased by the knowledge gained in the two preceding plays; their sufferings are caused by the selfish cruelty of Odysseus and the weakness of Agamemnon, which have both been demonstrated in the second play. The prophetess Kassandra, who was not believed by the Trojans in the first play when she foretold that the preservation of Paris would cause the disastrous Trojan War, is equally unheeded in the last play when she foresees the wanderings of Odysseus and the murder of Agamemnon. Hekabe, who in the first play weeps for her lost baby Paris and is wildly happy at his discovery, in this play has lost her husband and all her sons and performs the funeral rites for her grandson, Hektor's baby, Astyanax. And finally the unexpected appearance of Helen to have her self-defense torn into shreds by Hekabe is entirely right because the first play ended with the prophecy of her marriage to Paris.

In his next three productions[4] Euripides balances the first play against the second and makes the third an epilogue of a different kind. The *Antigone* and *Iphigenia in Tauris* were both plays about women which ended happily, and the *Hercules* is primarily about

---

[3] Cf. T. B. L. Webster, *Hermathena* 100 (1965): 21 ff.

[4] On the chronology see T. B. L. Webster, *Wiener Studien*, 79 (1966): 112 ff.

a man and ends unhappily. In 412 B.C. the *Andromeda* and *Helen* are variants on the theme rescue of distressed lady in exotic country, and the third play, *Ion*, has a more bitter flavor. The *Antiope* and *Hypsipyle* are both about the discovery of lost mothers by grown-up twin sons and end happily; the *Phoenissae*, which was probably produced with them, is about the two sons of Oedipus, who kill each other in battle before Thebes. But here, as in the Trojan trilogy, the plays are also linked by subject matter; the *Hypsipyle* is an incident in the expedition which culminates in the *Phoenissae*, and the *Antiope* is an earlier chapter in the history of Thebes. Still later in 407 B.C. the production in Macedonia seems to have comprised the *Temenus*, *Temenidae*, and *Archelaus*. In the first play the two bad elder sons of Temenos expelled Archelaos and murdered their father; in the second play they plotted against their brother-in-law, Deiphontes; and in the third play the good son, Archelaos, after various vicissitudes founded the kingdom of Macedonia—three chapters in the story of a single family.

The two earlier productions for which we have a complete list of plays, 438 and 431 B.C., show an entirely different principle of selection: the three plays are both different in kind and belong to a different cycle of legend. In 438 the *Cretan Women* dealt with Aerope's seduction of Thyestes and the grisly revenge taken by her elderly husband Atreus; in the *Alcmaeon in Psophis* Alkmaion betrayed his wife Arsinoe, who nevertheless remained loyal to him; the *Telephus* is an exciting camp play, which ends with the healing of the wounded Telephos in return for his promise to guide the Greeks to Troy. In 431 Euripides followed the same general pattern—a play about a bad woman, Medeia, who murdered her husband's new wife and then her own children; a play about an unhappy woman, Danae, who had to endure the unwanted attentions of the king, Polydektes; and a play about men, the *Philoktetes*. If, bearing these principles in mind, we inspect the plays which on metrical or other grounds can be allotted to Euripides' first nine productions, 455–428 B.C., it seems very likely that each production contained one play about a bad woman and one play about a suffering woman.

Three of the plays about bad women are about Medeia, (*Peliades*, *Aegeus*, *Medea*). The other six are about wives dissatisfied with their elderly husbands and throwing themselves at a young

lover, *Cretan Women, Phoenix, Stheneboea, Peleus, Hippolytus I and II.*
The two Hippolytos plays are of great interest because we can see
to a certain extent how Euripides remodeled his earlier play, of
which we only have fragments, to make the second play, which
survives complete. In the first play Theseus is away from Athens,
and his wife Phaidra has fallen in love with her stepson Hippolytos.
The following seems to me the probable outline. Phaidra sends the
Nurse to tempt Hippolytos. He rejects her; he is dedicated to the
clean life of the athlete. Phaidra then tempts him herself, and
Hippolytos covers his head in shame and throws away his sword,
which she has clutched, as a polluted object. Theseus returns to
find Phaidra threatening suicide with the sword, which he recognizes as belonging to Hippolytos; she tells him that Hippolytos has
tried to seduce her. He uses Poseidon's gift of a magic wish to curse
Hippolytos. Hippolytos is brought on dead, and Phaidra commits
suicide, probably because Theseus has now extracted the truth
from the nurse.

In the revised play Phaidra is quite different. She tries to sup-
press and conceal her passion; but the story must go on. Hippolytos must be accused, or Theseus cannot curse him. The nurse
extracts the truth from Phaidra and approaches Hippolytos.
Phaidra overhears Hippolytos storming at the nurse and sees him
leave the palace to wait for Theseus' return. Phaidra decides on
suicide. It is at this point that the chorus take refuge in "the
Apple-tree, the singing, and the gold." Theseus returns to find
Phaidra dead with a tablet in her hand which accuses Hippolytos
of seducing her. In this way she feels she can help her children by
preserving her own reputation. Theseus curses Hippolytos, who
arrives at this moment and defends himself; here Euripides has
bought our sympathy for Phaidra at the price of Hippolytos; in
the first play Hippolytos defends his celibate athleticism to the
nurse and possibly to Phaidra herself; here his defense is unsym-
pathetic because it is made to his widowed and desolate father
after the much more sympathetic Phaidra has committed suicide.
Euripides makes some amends by the later heartbreaking dialogue
with Artemis, who tells Theseus the truth. Brilliantly, Euripides
hypostatizes Hippolytos' dedication to athletics in Artemis, the
goddess of hunting, and Phaidra's disastrous passion in Aphrodite,
who speaks the prologue. This is how they themselves feel the
forces that drive them, and this justifies a device, which Euripides

had probably already used to explain Pasiphae's passion for the bull in the *Cretans* and was to use later devastatingly in the *Bacchae*.

An ancient scholar says that Euripides corrected in the second play what was unseemly and worthy of accusation in the first play. We know that the comic poets called three of the early unsatisfied wives, Aerope, Stheneboia, and the first Phaidra, by the rudest word they could find, "whores"; they must have appeared unseemly and worthy of accusation because Euripides stripped these legendary heroines of their Aeschylean splendor and presented them as fifth-century Athenians, and this is what Sophocles meant by saying that Euripides "presented people as they are." But, as we shall see, Euripides, so far from heeding the criticism and abandoning his formula, extended its application in his later plays. The new Phaidra is not less realistic; she is different, and the question is, Why?

Mr. Barrett[5] thinks of Sophocles' *Phaedra* as an answer to Euripides' *Hippolytus I* and itself answered by *Hippolytus II*. This is very tempting, as the fragments suggest that Sophocles' Phaedra had the excuse that she thought Theseus was dead; she really believed that Aphrodite's power was invincible; she used a go-between to approach Hippolytos instead of throwing herself at his head; and she may have accused Hippolytos to save her own children. Euripides took over the indirect approach to Hippolytos and the motivation of her later accusation, but denied her the excuse that Theseus was in Hades, and transformed Aphrodite from a venerable goddess into a hypostatization of Phaidra's passion. To whitewash Phaidra partly by making her make a pardonable mistake, partly by pseudo-religion, partly by reducing Hippolytos' part (a reasonable deduction from Sophocles' title, *Phaedra*) must have seemed to him too easy a way out. That Sophocles could take such a way out is shown by his treatment of Deianeira in the contemporary *Trachiniae*.

Professor Bruno Snell[6] has supposed a sort of dialogue between Euripides and Socrates. Medeia in 431 B.C. said "I know what evil I am going to do, but passion is stronger than my reasoning." Socrates answered that if you know what is right, then you do it. Phaidra comes back in 428 B.C.: "We know what is right and

---

[5] *Euripides: Hippolytos* (Oxford, 1964), pp. 12 ff.

[6] *Scenes from Greek Drama* (Berkeley, 1964), pp. 59 ff.

recognize it, but we do not work it out, some from laziness, others putting some other pleasure before the good." This is not, I think, a debate between Euripides and Socrates, but Euripides making his characters explain themselves in Socratic terminology. At the end of his life in the *Iphigenia in Aulis* (558ff.) he makes the chorus sing: "men may differ in nature and behavior. But the truly right is always clear. Education greatly contributes to virtue. Modesty is wisdom, and has the exceeding grace of perceiving the right by force of intellect." This is the Socratic position, and they then glance back at Phaidra's problem and judge her: "It is a great thing to pursue virtue—for women in secret love." It is interesting that just about the time when Euripides was writing the *Medea* and *Hippolytus II* the comic poets were saying that Socrates helped him to write his tragedies. They too saw the influence of Socrates on his dramatization of the struggle between passion and reason, evident in Medeia and the second Phaidra but appearing also in a different form in Alkmene in the *Heraclidae* and Hekabe in her name play.

Although the position of Sophocles' *Phaedra* between Euripides' two versions of the story must remain a guess, we have evidence for a later sequence of plays, which will also show how Euripides developed the use of his formula. The way in which Aristophanes quotes Aeschylus' *Choephori* in the second edition of the *Clouds*, which was produced between 421 and 416 B.C., shows both that the *Choephori* had been recently revived and that Euripides had not yet produced his *Electra*, which on metrical grounds must be dated before 416 B.C. Sophocles' *Electra* must be later than Euripides' *Electra* and before Euripides' *Helen* of 412 B.C. Euripides' *Orestes* was produced in 408 B.C. The sequence ran therefore: revival of Aeschylus' *Choephori*, Euripides' *Electra*, Sophocles' *Electra*, Euripides' *Orestes*.

Aeschylus' *Choephori* was sandwiched between his *Agamemnon*—in which Agamemnon returned from Troy to be murdered by his wife Klytemnestra—and his *Eumenides*, in which Orestes was acquitted at Athens of the murder of his mother. The other two dramatists had to write an *Electra* which was complete in itself. In Aeschylus, Orestes arrives back from exile just as Elektra is being sent to pour libations on Agamemnon's grave because Klytemnestra has had an ominous dream. Elektra recognizes him by the hair which he has put on Agamemnon's grave and by his footprint. He tells his sister that Apollo has prophesied terrible tortures if he does not kill his father's murderess. The center of the play is a long lyric dialogue between Orestes, Elektra, and the chorus, in which they invoke the dead Agamemnon to nerve Orestes for his deed. Then Elektra vanishes from the action. Orestes is admitted by Klytemnestra because he says he has brought the news of Orestes' death. Aigisthos is summoned and goes in to be killed. Then, wavering and strengthened at the last moment by Pylades' only utterance in the play, Orestes drives Klytemnestra in to be killed. As he stands over the corpse, he sees the avenging Furies of his mother and rushes from the stage.

Euripides modernizes. The great lyric invocation of the dead King which takes more than 200 lines in Aeschylus is reduced to 13 lines of very effective prayer (*El.* 671 ff.); nor can Apollo be so closely present (he is actually a character in Aeschylus' third play). In one minor point Euripides says clearly what he is doing: the Aeschylean Elektra recognizes Orestes by family hair and family foot; the Euripidean Elektra says "nonsense: a young athlete has his hair cut short, and a woman's hair is soft and long; a man's foot is much bigger than a woman's." We are firmly transferred from heroic legend to contemporary town life. He asks what would Klytemnestra and Aigisthos do with these uncomfortable children who remembered their father; put a price on the boy's head (he remembered his own earlier *Cresphontes* here) and marry off the girl to a poor farmer who will not be dangerous. So here, as in the earlier *Diktys*, the princess is living in a poor man's hut instead of the palace (perhaps he also remembered Mandane in Herodotus).

This change of setting involved a complete remodeling of the two murders. Euripides has, however, gained the moving picture of the poor farmer who respects Elektra and whose friendship she values, however embittered she feels toward her mother and stepfather. Orestes enters with Pylades (who is mute all through this play) and watches Elektra return with her waterpot and the chorus meet her with an invitation to go to a festival of Hera—the married Elektra fetching the household water instead of the Aeschylean Elektra sent by Klytemnestra to pour libations, and the opening chorus transposing an everyday occasion into lyric phantasy, as in the *Hippolytus*. Elektra describes to the unrecognized Orestes her misery, the luxurious life of Klytemnestra, and Aigisthos dancing drunk on Agamemnon's tomb. The farmer returns and invites the strangers in; Orestes is deeply disturbed by the contrast between honest poverty and corrupt wealth. Elektra sends her husband to ask an old servant of Agamemnon to bring food for the guests. He arrives with a lamb, cheeses, and wine; he recognizes Orestes by a scar on his brow. Then the plan is made (and this is entirely new); the old man is first to take Orestes to where Aigisthos is sacrificing (here again Euripides borrows from his own *Cresphontes*) and then to tell Klytemnestra that Elektra had a baby ten days ago and needs her help.

A messenger reports Aigisthos' death, and Orestes comes back carrying his head, over which Elektra vents her hatred: "you killed my father and married my mother. Then you found you had married a tyrant, and you had to amuse yourself by running after girls." (This Aigisthos reminds us of the husbands of later Greek comedy.) Klytemnestra is seen in the distance. Orestes nearly breaks down: "Apollo, your oracle is a great folly," "Was it an evil spirit spoke in the guise of god?" Elektra tells him not to be a coward and sends him in to wait for Klytemnestra. She arrives in a chariot attended by Trojan captives. She defends her murder of Agamemnon, and Elektra tears her defense to pieces. But she has come to help Elektra sacrifice. "Come into my humble home. Take care my sooty house does not dirty your frock. You shall make the sacrifice you ought."

After the murder the two come out bitterly repentant. Elektra accepts the responsibility which the chorus lays on her: "you did a terrible wrong to your brother and forced his will." The Dioskoroi appear on the *mechane* to finish the play. "Apollo is wise but his oracle was not wisdom for you," "the unwise cries of Apollo's tongue." However Pylades will marry Elektra and establish the farmer in Phokis, and Orestes after being pursued by the Furies will be acquitted in Athens.

Euripides has pushed Apollo into the background. Orestes at the crisis has doubts of the oracle, and the Dioskoroi imply at best that it has been misinterpreted. It is Elektra who both plans the murder of Klytemnestra and nerves Orestes to carry it out. Klytemnestra is a snobbish, domineering, vulgar woman; Aigisthos, although we only see his severed head, comes out clearer than in Aeschylus or Sophocles as a vicious young opportunist. Elektra and Orestes are not much better than their mother, but at least they appreciate the loyal friendship provided by Elektra's husband, the old man, and Pylades, and at least they repent.

These are people "as they are." Sophocles was moved to answer. For him the oracle given to Orestes must be the center of the story, and since Apollo cannot command anything that is wrong, Elektra and Orestes cannot repent and Orestes cannot be pursued by Furies. The problem is to present matricide as an act of justice, and to make it tolerable on the stage. The answer is masterly: minimize the matricide and Orestes' part, blacken Klytemnestra, and make the audience identify themselves with Elektra so that they see the matricide with her eyes. This Elektra has lived on in the palace, persecuted by Klytemnestra, who showers favor on the fluffy sister Chrysothemis because she accepts the situation. Elektra is on stage from the end of the prologue, and the climax of the play is her vast upsurge of joy when Orestes reveals himself to her, very late in the play, *after* she has been shattered by the false report of his death. Then the murders are slipped in at the end: after the recognition scene Orestes goes into the house and dispatches Klytemnestra; Aigisthos arrives and is driven in to die where he had killed Agamemnon. Nothing could be more efficient; we have seen Klytemnestra's defense of her past destroyed by Elektra, we have heard her pray to Apollo for the destruction of her own children, we have heard her joy at the report of Orestes' death; but from that moment we are entirely concerned with Elektra's despair at the report, Elektra's desperate appeal to Chrysothemis for help, Elektra's utter desolation when Orestes enters with what purports to be his own funeral urn, Elektra's joy when he reveals himself. We do not see Klytemnestra again: no pathetic appeal to Orestes as in Aeschylus; no commiseration with Elektra's poverty just before the murder and no heartbroken description of her last moments as in Euripides; just a cry off stage.

Gilbert Murray has been criticized for calling the Sophoclean *Electra* a "combination of matricide and high spirits," but that is exactly how Euripides must have seen the play. The Sophoclean Orestes falters for a moment, not because he has to murder his mother but because he cannot bear Elektra's grief; otherwise he is cheerful and efficient, but Sophocles very cleverly allows him to be on stage a little over half as long as the Euripidean Orestes, so that we do not care much about him. Euripides could not accept this and in the *Orestes* of 408 B.C. asks what happened next. In his *Electra* the Dioskoroi see the Furies coming to chase Orestes (κύνας τάσδε); Euripides has accepted for his epilogue the Aeschylean ending to the story since one of the functions of the epilogue is to get the characters back into traditional mythology. In the *Orestes* the scene is the palace five days after the murders. Elektra speaks the prologue. Orestes is in bed starving, but asleep during a respite from his intermittent madness, in which he sees Furies. The city will decide today whether they are to die by stoning. Their only hope is Menelaos, who has already sent Helen secretly into the palace; their daughter, Hermione, has been there for the duration of the Trojan War. Helen is afraid to take offerings to Klytemnestra's tomb; Elektra refuses and tells her to send Hermione. The chorus of Argive women come to ask for news, and Elektra is terrified that they will wake Orestes. Orestes wakes and Elektra tends him, but he has another mad fit and thinks she is a Fury trying to hurl him to hell. He recovers, and in a very moving dialogue doubts whether Agamemnon himself would have approved his action: now brother and sister have only their mutual loyalty and love. Menelaos arrives and Orestes pleads for his help. But he is cut short by Tyndareus, the father of Klytemnestra and Helen, who says that Orestes ought not to have killed his mother but to have prosecuted her; he is going to plead with the Argives to put the murderers to death. Menelaos says that he will wait until the people have calmed down before he tries to put in a word for Orestes (and does not even appear at the trial). The meter changes to recitative trochaics for Pylades, the loyal friend who has been banished from home for his part in the murder and now comes to persuade Orestes to defend himself at the trial. The trial is reported to Elektra: all that Orestes could achieve was permission for himself and Elektra to take their own lives. Orestes and Pylades return, and the three movingly talk of suicide. But Pylades suggests that they should first murder Helen, and Elektra says that they can seize Hermione as a hostage. Then follows the frenzied sequence of scenes which has already been described leading up to the final tableau and the appearance of Apollo.

Sophocles neatly avoided the consequences of matricide. Aeschylus saw the acquittal of Orestes as a step forward in civilization: the solemn establishment of the first murder court by Athena with Apollo as witness and the Furies as prosecutor. Euripides reports what might be a contemporary debate: Talthybios, Agamemnon's herald, sides with the friends of Aigisthos. Diomedes suggests banishment instead of death. A popular orator with doubtful credentials urges stoning in a speech which was inspired by Tyndareus. An honest farmer says that Orestes ought to be crowned for killing a bad woman (did Euripides mean to have us remember the poor farmer who was married to Elektra?) Finally Orestes pleads that if wives are allowed to kill their husbands, men will be either dead or slaves.

Euripides sees not only the trial but the whole story as a contemporary situation. The murder of Klytemnestra has everyday consequences for her whole family: for her son and daughter and his friend Pylades, for her father Tyndareus, for her sister Helen (who is so like her), and for her brother-in-law Menelaos (who is so like the dead Agamemnon). The same family reappears in the posthumous *Iphigeneia in Aulis:* Agamemnon; Menelaos; Klytemnestra; Iphigeneia, Klytemnestra's dower-slave; and Achilles, the supposed fiancé of Iphigeneia. Menelaos, Klytemnestra, and the dower-slave at least are surely additions by Euripides to the story. So too in the *Phoenissae*, which was produced two or three years before the *Orestes*, and perhaps soon after a revival of Aeschylus *Seven against Thebes* in the form in which we now have it, Eteokles' lust for power is shown to affect the whole royal family, his brother Polyneikes, his sister Antigone, his mother Iokaste, his father Oidipous, his uncle Kreon, and his cousin Menoikeus, who all have their parts, as well as the old family seer Teiresias. Even in the posthumous *Bacchae*, where the influence of the traditional resistance story must have been extremely strong, the pragmatical Kadmos, who sees the political advantage of having a god in the family, and the modernist churchman Teiresias, who explains a miracle by philology, are surely Euripidean additions. And who before could have put on the stage either Kadmos the father nursing his daughter back to sanity or Kadmos the grandfather praising after the disaster his errant grandson?

Both the plots and the characters of the late plays seem to me to correspond to the changed metrical texture which I described earlier. The action is no longer dominated and directed by a small number of strong characters but advances falteringly under the influence of family intimacy, family quarrels, family likeness, family diversity, and for this the more complicated metrical texture is admirably adapted. The characters themselves, some of them at least, are less stable in the later plays: the beginning lies in the split personality of Phaidra and the suicidal repentance of the vengeful Hermione in the *Andromache*, but consider later Herakles' confident strength followed by his destructive madness and then by his restoration to sanity by Theseus, the gentle heart-broken Kreousa changing into an inefficient murderess, or the physically starved and mentally crazed Orestes turning into an efficient criminal. They need the shimmer of the late iambics and the full range through recitative to untrammelled lyric to express their instability.

Apollo at the end of the *Orestes* announces the future: Orestes will go to Athens and be acquitted. He will come back and marry Hermione (at whose neck he is at the moment pointing his sword). Elektra will marry Pylades. Menelaos will retire to Sparta. Helen will be honored as a goddess. Pirandello would have left his audience to decide what happened next: Euripides uses Apollo to put the derailed characters back on their mythological tramlines. Why does he think this desirable?

Consistently with his formula of modernization, his people can quote modern interpretations of legend. The chorus in the *Iphigenia in Aulis* wonder whether the story of Leda and the Swan may not be merely a figment of poetry. Iphigeneia in the *Iphigenia in Tauris* does not believe that Artemis likes human sacrifice: the local inhabitants have ascribed their own murderous tendencies to their goddess. When Helen in the *Trojan Women* defends herself by the judgment of Paris and says that Aphrodite came with Paris to abduct her, Hekabe answers: "Nonsense. My son was very handsome, and your mind seeing him became Aphrodite." As in the *Hippolytus*, Aphrodite is a hypostatization of sexual desire, although this interpretation here destroys the whole mythological framework of the trilogy. In the *Hercules* Theseus administers the conventional consolation, that if the gods in spite of their transgressions live in Olympus a mortal should equally be able to endure his sins and misfortunes; Herakles answers: "I do not believe that the gods indulge in rape or imprison one another. These are the figments of singers." Again the whole play is based on Zeus' seduction of Alkmene and Hera's anger thereat, a framework which Herakles' insight shatters. The surprising thing is that Euripides generally puts the pieces together again.

Two possible reasons (apart from tradition) can be suggested. One is that Euripides believed that cult had a value at least for ordinary people, and cult could not be wholly divorced from mythology. The chorus of the *Bacchae* need not necessarily reflect Euripides when he makes it say: "What the ordinary crowd believe, I would accept." But it is remarkable that, even with our insufficient knowledge, we can say that in eighteen plays certainly, and in five others probably, Euripides expressly connected his story, generally at the end of the play but sometimes earlier, with an existing cult, holy grave, or temple. Medeia in her jealous fury has murdered her children, but their tombs will be honored forever in Perachora; Herakles has denied conventional mythology, but after his death the Athenians will honor him with sacrifices and shrines. Euripides, however much he innovates, refuses to cut the traditional link between mythology and cult.

The other reason has been given already. Traditional mythology is a world of beautiful phantasy. Chorus and characters can escape into it; the audience appreciate it as a foil to the realism of modern interpretation. Euripides was too good a poet to abandon completely "the Apple-Tree, the singing, and the gold."

Victor Pöschl

❧ POETRY AND PHILOSOPHY IN HORACE

The poetry of Horace stems from the deep experience of a dreadful catastrophe: the collapse of the order of state and life at the end of the Roman republic. This collapse occurred in a relentless sequence of murderous civil wars. The works of Augustan poetry are real *fleurs du mal*, blossoms that grow out of evil. They are the answer of the Roman mind to this challenge, the result of the meeting of subtle sensibility and fearsome threat.

The most famous testimony of Horace's despair as to the fate of Rome is one of his earliest poems, the Sixteenth Epode. In this poem there is an apocalyptic mood. Wild animals are to take possession of the Roman soil. Barbarians will come to the ruins of Rome and the bones of Romulus will be scattered to the four winds.[1]

In the face of such distress, the poet turns to the "pious" who are ready to sail with him to the islands of the blessed, which he describes in verses of magical beauty. Jupiter preserved the Golden Age for the pious when he introduced the Bronze Age in this world. The land of the blessed in the Western Sea[2] is a symbol of the longing of Horace's time for a guiltless and peaceful existence, a "pious"

---

[1] A similar eschatological tone is sounded in the Sibylline oracles of the same age (*Oracula Sibyllina* III, 464–69, p. 72 Geffcken): "Italy, not from without does Ares, the God of War, come to you. No, native bloodshed, much lamented, will destroy you. You will be laid in ashes and unawares you will tear your own flesh; you will be not mother of good men, but wet nurse of wild animals."

[2] For some aspects of this idea in connection with America, see Harold Jantz, "The Myths about America: Origins and Extensions," *Jahrbuch für Amerikastudien* 5 (1962): 10 ff.

47

world, separated by an ocean from the impure, contaminated
world of contemporary Rome.

From the darkness of his age the poet leads us into a better
world. The pastorals of Vergil, written a little before this epode,
have the same purpose: they lead us in a realm of peace, philan-
thropy, love and freedom. Vergil and Horace attempt to fulfill the
claim of Greek philosophy: deliverance and redemption of man
from his sorrows and pains, from his wrong opinions, from his
misconception of what true life is.[3] The center of man's existence
is shifting from the political universe to a private life that carries
its value and its legitimacy in itself. Thus Horace becomes the
creator of a personal culture.

The great Greek name giving this shift its philosophical foundation is Epicurus. He was the Greek philosopher who made legiti-
mate the Roman evolution toward individualism and individual
culture. Epicurean philosophy thus plays a very great part in
Rome.

The shift from the political to the personal, from flaunting
splendor to the simple and unpretentious, is a main theme of
Horace's poems, not only in their content, but also in their form
and their inner movement. If we let ourselves be guided by the
magic power of this movement, which has the effect of music for a
sensitive mind, we are introduced spontaneously into this world of
peace, of happiness, of quiet detachment. The poet, as it were,
conquers this world anew in each poem.

The political realm, the universe of the Roman Empire, with the
sublime names of foreign nations and kings, is contrasted with the
world of the poet. Though small, it is filled with light and happiness. We have this movement, for instance, in the charming Ode
I, 26:

> Dear to the Muses, I will banish gloom and fear to the wild winds to
> carry o'er the Cretan Sea, all unconcerned what ruler of the frozen
> borders of the North is object of our fear, or what dangers frighten
> Tiridates.
> Do thou, sweet Muse, that takest joy in fountains fresh, weave gay
> blossoms, yea, weave them as a garland for my Lamia! Naught with-
> out thee avail my tributes. Him in new measures, him with Lesbian
> plectrum, 'tis meet that thou and thy sisters should make immortal.[4]

[3] V. Pöschl, *Die Hirtendichtung Virgils* (Heidelberg, 1964).
[4] Translation by C. E. Bennett in the Loeb Classical Library.

Or the Ode II, 11:

What the warlike Cantabrian is plotting, Quinctius Hirpinus, and the Scythian, divided from us by the intervening Adriatic, cease to inquire, and be not anxious for the needs of life, since 'tis little that it asks. Fresh youth and beauty are speeding fast away behind us, while wizened age is banishing sportive love and slumbers soft. Not forever do the flowers of spring retain their glory, nor does blushing Luna shine always with the selfsame face. Why, with planning for the future, weary thy soul unequal to the task? Why not rather quaff the wine, while yet we may, reclining under this lofty plane or pine, in careless ease, our grey locks garlanded with fragrant roses and perfumed with Syrian nard? Bacchus dispels carking cares. What slave will swiftly temper the bowls of fiery Falernian with water from the passing stream? Who will lure from her home Lyde, coy wench? With ivory lyre, come bid her haste, her careless hair fastened in a knot, like some Laconian maid.[5]

We have the same movement, again, in those poems where the splendid, ostentatious way of life is rejected, as in the prayer to the Palatine Apollo in the Ode I, 31. The poet does not pray for the rich harvests of fertile Sardinia, for warm Calabria's pleasant herds, nor gold nor Indian ivory . . . "Olives nourish me and light mallow," the most common food. The Ode closes with these lines:

Oh, grant me, Phoebus, calm content,
Strength unimpaired, a mind entire
Old age without dishonor spent,
Nor unbefriended by the lyre.[6]

The Ode I, 7, *Laudabunt alii*, one of the most beautiful, belongs to this group also. "Let others praise bright Rhodes and Mytilene and Ephesos and Corinth, Thebes, Delphi. . . . Nothing delights me so much as the grottoes of Albunea that to the Anio re-echo, the Anio which rushes into the depths." To the magnificence of the Greek world is contrasted the simple and beloved countryside of Tivoli. As the song reaches this point, the poet exhorts his friend Munatius Plancus to soften his sorrows with mild wine. It seems as if he should be drawn into the consoling and healing realm of the poet, symbolized by Tivoli. But then it seems, the friend will continue to suffer even when in Tivoli. In the face of this distress and weariness, Horace cites the mythical example of the Greek

---

[5] *Ibid.*

[6] Translation by John Conington in *The Odes and Carmen Saeculare of Horace Translated by John Conington* (3rd ed.; London, 1865), p. 32.

hero Teucer, who when struck by a particularly harsh blow, nevertheless bore his fate with serene composure. After ten years of
heavy struggles at Troy, where he had left his brother Ajax, killed
in the war, Teucer had gone home to Salamis. There his father
Telamon cast him off and expelled him, angry because he had not
taken better care of his brother. But Teucer did not lose his spirits.
As he exhorted his comrades to come with him on the ship again,
to entrust themselves to fate, and not to despair, he says:

> "Now let us drive away sorrows with wine, tomorrow we shall cross
> again the immense sea."

> Nunc vino pellite curas,
> cras ingens iterabimus aequor.

Thus, the Ode closes with the exhortation to look gladly to the
present, even when tomorrow we must cross the mighty waters.[7]

The tragic fate of Teucer, who after long years sees again his
beloved native country and then is expelled again and forever—a
fate to which Sophocles and Pacuvius had given form in famous
tragedies—is a fate typical of the age. How many, like Teucer, lost
their native country after long years of absence at the very moment
when they believed they had found it again. How many of those
who fought for Brutus and the cause of the republic came home
to find their land expropriated. Horace was one of those who
suffered in this way, for his father's lands had been taken away.

In the great poems of the Augustan Age we meet time and again
the fate of homelessness, of being expelled, of men finding themselves as if before an abyss. I might recall the first pastoral of Vergil
and the *Aeneid*, for both of which the basic theme is the search for
a new home.

In the words "Drive away sorrows with wine, tomorrow we will
cross the immense sea," something is revealed that is central for
the poetry of Horace. His anacreontic serenity stands before a
tragic background: the cruel visions of death and all kinds of
anxieties, sorrows, and pain that Horace and his friends had expe-
rienced in the impressionable years of their youth. It is not an easy
composure that is demanded, but one full of tension and effort,
one that must be regained time and again.

So the movement of the poem proves to be a gradual concentra-

---

[7] This is a lyrical, epicurean transformation of the famous words, spoken by Odysseus
in the sea-storm, imitated by Vergil in the first book of the *Aeneid*.

tion, a gradual narrowing and tightening in the direction of what matters most, of what is most essential. The poem begins serenely and broadly with the splendidly displayed names of Greek towns. Then the splendor gathers, as it were, in one point: in the beloved small town of Tivoli. But then it appears that even this place of seclusion is not necessary for happiness. Even the expelled, the homeless, the man exposed to an unknown fate (brightened, it is true, by the oracle of Apollo), the hero who must leave even Salamis, the poorest of all islands—contrasted purposely with the famous places of the bright beginning—can still enjoy the present hour. From nothing a moment of happiness can grow, and in the face of this moment everything else vanishes. Everything else sinks down before the one thing that remains: the man who knows how to grasp the present with composure.

The same movement toward the essential is to be found in a very famous ode, that has been treated—and mistreated, as I believe—very often in the last years: the Soracte Ode (I,9).[8] It is the first song in the collection of odes written in the Alcaic meter, and this gives the poem a certain prominence: it is an homage to the Greek poet Alcaeus whom Horace chose above all as a model for his lyric poetry.

The poem begins with the picture of winter: the mountain Soracte covered with deep snow, the trees laboring under their burden, the rivers frozen with the sharp cold. This is not the expression of a state of soul and not a symbol of old age.[9] It is the Roman winter and nothing else. I think today one looks too much for symbols. The friend of poetry may enjoy the pleasure of continuing the work of the poet and adding his own poetry. But the philologist has to listen to the poet and to perceive carefully what he says. This is harder than we think, as in life listening accurately is an art mastered only by few.

Against the cold of winter there is help: a good fire and Sabine wine. But there are "other things"—*cetera*—likely to alarm us, things that make our hearts heavy. What can we do against these things? "Leave them to the gods": *Permitte divis cetera.* "Once they

---

[8] For a closer analysis of the poem, see V. Pöschl, "Die Soracteode des Horaz," *Wiener Studien*, 79 (1966): 365–83.

[9] For the opposite view, see L. P. Wilkinson, *Horace and His Lyric Poetry* (Cambridge, 1951), pp. 130 f.; and Steele Commager, *The Odes of Horace* (New Haven–London, 1962), p. 271.

have laid low the winds battling to the end with the seething ocean, then neither the cypresses nor the old ashes are shaken any more."

The storms are a metaphor for the adversities of life we cannot avoid, political and private disturbances, that cause fear, sorrow and suffering. The consolation offered by the poet is: these things will pass as storms pass. Some interpreters believe that here the poet points to the calm of death.[10] They are certainly wrong. Death for Horace is the inescapable necessity[11] that gives every happy moment of this life its value, but never is death in Horace a consolation, as it is in Cicero or Seneca or even in Lucretius.

From the unpleasant things compared with storms the poet quite naturally passes to the central exhortation, that here appears for the first time in the collection of the odes: "Do not ask what to-morrow will bring" (*Quid sit futurum cras, fuge quaerere*) "and set down as gain each day that Chance will give" (*Quem fors dierum cumque dabit, lucro appone*). That does not mean only: each day you live is a gain. The poet points to the Epicurean balance sheet: we must try to gather more happy hours and days in our life than unhappy ones and must not poison them by sad thoughts. We must attempt to make the most out of life, "as long as gloomy grey age is far from green youth" (*Donec virenti canities abest morosa*). "As long as you are young, seek the Campus Martius and the squares" (*Nunc et campus et areae*), not as many interpreters since Giorgio Pasquali[12] believe in order to indulge in love on squares at night— that would be indeed a bit inappropriate to such a season—but to sport: riding, ball games and so on, for which the Campus Martius and the *areae* are the indicated places. Love is mentioned only after that: "Seek soft whispers at the appointed hour of nightfall: now seek the laugh that betrays the girl hiding in a secret corner and the pledge snatched from her arm or finger scarcely resisting":

> lenesque sub nocem susurri
> composita repetantur hora,
>
> nunc et latentis proditor intimo
> gratus puellae risus ab angulo
> pignusque dereptum lacertis
> aut digito male pertinaci.

---

[10] Wilkinson and Commager, *ll.cc.*

[11] *Necessitas. Odes* III, 1, 14: *aequa lege Necessitas sortitur insignes et imos.*

[12] G. Pasquali, *Orazio lirico* (Firenze, 1920), p. 83.

Three antitheses are contained in the poem: the antithesis between the winter and the pleasant banquet with cosy fire and good wine; the antithesis between the storms that bother us, the end of which we must wait for with patience and acquiescence; the antithesis between old age and youth and its joys.

The last stanza belongs entirely to the pleasures of love, wooing and seduction, the gesture of flight and provocative hiding and resisting that are natural feminine expressions of the wish for love.

Thus, we have three steps:

1. the pleasure of a cosy banquet, enhanced as it were by the cold outdoors;
2. the reasonable consideration that every bad thing will pass, followed by the general exhortation of the poet to grasp the moment;
3. the unqualified abandonment to the happy moment of love and expectation of love.

In the last stanzas all things and thoughts evoked by the poet vanish. A cone of light falls on the happy innocent scene of love described in charming details. In the movement of the poem itself, the poet shows us how to put away the gloomy sides of life and how to indulge entirely in the present: the essential reality of life according to Horace and to some modern philosophers. Thus the poem becomes in a way philosophy in action. At its end only the happy moment is present. All threatening matters seem to have disappeared. Have they really? I think old age is present in the person of the poet, in so far as he is supposed to be an elderly man. So the happiness in which the poem culminates is at the same time the poet's recollection of the happy times of youth. This recollection, the awareness of having lived, is happiness too, as the poet states in the great poem that unfolds in a most magnificent manner the main motifs of the Soracte Ode: the Ode to Maecenas (III, 29): *Tyrrhena regum*.[13] In this ode, the poet, with the same conjuring gesture and the same magic of musical movement, turns to Maecenas. He invites his friend to leave Rome and to come to his country house, where vine, roses, and fragrant ointment await

[13] For a fuller interpretation, see V. Pöschl, "Die grosse Maecenasode des Horaz (c.3,29)," *Sitzungsberichte der Heidelberger Akademie der Wissenschaften* (*phil.-hist Klasse*), 1961, Abhandlung 1.

the noble guest. Maecenas is asked not to hesitate any longer, to get up quickly, and to come: *eripe te morae.* Here sounds a tone that has much significance in this poem. We must not put off living. The invitation becomes an exhortation to change our lives. We are near the Epicurean wisdom: "We are born only once. It is not possible to be born twice. For all eternity I shall not exist. You are not the master of tomorrow's day, yet you put off always what brings joy. Life passes in procrastination and everyone dies without having found leisure."[14]

In the following stanzas Horace confronts the peace of the rural summer with the political sorrows of Maecenas. As in the First Eclogue of Vergil, the bucolic realm of peace is contrasted with the political world of sorrows, a realm where time stands still and only the blissful present rules. The center of the poem contains these lines (III, 29, 29–45):

> "With wise purpose does the god bury in the shades of night the future's outcome, and laughs if mortals be anxious beyond due limits. Remember to settle with tranquil heart the problem of the hour! All else is borne along like some river, now gliding peacefully in midchannel into the Tuscan Sea, now rolling polished stones, uprooted trees, and flocks and homes together, with echoing of the hills and neighboring woods, while the wild deluge stirs up the peaceful streams. Master of himself and joyful will that man live who day be day can say: 'I have lived today; tomorrow let the Father fill the heaven with murky clouds or radiant sunshine. Yet will he not render vain whatever is past, nor will he alter and undo what once the fleeting hour has brought.' "[15]

> prudens futuri temporis exitum
> caliginosa nocte premit deus
>   ridetque, si mortalis ultra
>   fas trepidat . . . quod adest memento
>
> componere aequos: cetera fluminis
> ritu feruntur, nunc medio aequore
>   cum pace delabentis Etruscum
>   in mare, nunc lapides adesos
>
> stirpesque raptas et pecus et domus
> volventis una non sine montium
>   clamore vicinaeque silvae
>   cum fera diluvies quietos

---

[14] *Gnomologium Vaticanum* 14 = C. Diano, *Epicuri Ethica,* 92, p. 58.
[15] Bennett's translation, Loeb Classical Library.

irritat amnes. ille potens sui
laetusque deget, cui licet in diem
dixisse "vixi: cras vel atra
nube polum pater occupato,

vel sole puro: non tamen irritum
quodcumque retro est, efficiet neque
diffinget infectumque reddet,
quod fugiens semel hora vexit."

"Remember to settle the problem of the hour." As in the famous
poem *Aequam memento* (*Odes*, II, 3), the well-balanced mind is revealed in living serenely for the present in the face of death. What
matters most is to fulfill life. This thought is expressed in the ode
Otium divos (II, 16) by means of mythological examples. With the
fulfilled brief life of Achilles is contrasted the life of the eternal old
man Tithonus. It is not sufficient to grasp the moment. Superficial
enjoyment is not meant, but the real fulfillment of time, as Lucretius says (III, 596): "Because you ever yearn for what is not present, and despise what is, life has slipped from your grasp unfinished
and unsatisfying." Every day, every hour, decides whether life is
"*vita perfecta*" or "*imperfecta*," fulfilled or unfulfilled. One of the
best formulations of fulfilled life we find in Seneca, in what I believe to be one of the most beautiful exhortations left to us from
antiquity: "A great artist shows himself by being able to include
the whole in small compass": *magni artificis est totum continuisse in
exiguo.*

To the present are opposed "the other things," "all else": the
cetera as in the Soracte Ode, all that is out of the present and not
in the power of man, the realm of politics and fate, where irrational
forces rule. "The other things" are seen in the image of the river,
symbol of the inexorable coming and going, of that which is exposed to a perpetual change, of mercilessly flowing time, of the
perishable—the extreme opposite of the fulfilled present.

But the wild untamed power of the river which whirls to ruin
trees and cattle and men's homes recoils, as it were, from the wise
man. In the middle of the line its power is broken as by a rock:
ille potens sui laetusque. To know that the moment really lived is im-
perishable gives man serene calm and independence from everything to come. Even God cannot destroy what has been. Here the

omnipotence of God has its limit. These words have something of a Promethean defiance. At the end of the poem Horace turns to himself:

> Fortune, exulting in her cruel work, and stubborn to pursue her wanton sport, shifts her fickle favours, kind now to me, now to some other. I praise her while she stays; but if she shake her wings for flight, I renounce her gifts, enwrap me in my virtue, and woo honest Poverty, undowered though she be. Not mine, when masts are groaning with the Afric gales, to have recourse to wretched prayers and with vows to strike a compact with the gods that my Cyprian and my Tyrian wares shall not add new riches to the devouring sea. Then the breezes and Pollux with his brother shall bear me through the tempest of the Aegean main, safely protected in my two oared lifeboat.

Poverty is the poet's bride, Virtue his cloak: that is playful and ironical, but none the less serious. It is the expression of the serene smile with which the poet looks on Fortune's raging. And behind Fortune's raging all the bitter experiences of the age are concealed. But the poet sails safely in a small lifeboat after the shipwreck, guided by kindly powers through the tempests of life. The gods protect him. As he says of himself in another poem, "The gods delight in me, my piety, my Muse" (*Odes* I, 17, 13–14).

> Di me tuentur, dis pietas mea
> et Musa cordi est.

Thus the poem ends in a religious realm. Two forms of religious attitude are contrasted: the miserable fear of the gods, which is only a disguised form of greed, the kind of religion condemned by Lucretius, and the personal religion of Horace, the pious faith that the realm of happiness disclosed by him is blessed by the gods. A miracle happens: the waves of the sea do no harm to the small lifeboat of the poet.

In this poem the decision in favor of a personal life full of simplicity and poverty is brought together with the friendship of Maecenas and Horace. This friendship of the minister of the Emperor with the poet is based on the generous recognition which the powerful man seems to give to the poet's decisively proclaimed ideal of an unpolitical personal life. But this does not mean that Horace did not have to struggle for his liberty. Many a poem, especially in the *Satires* and *Epistles*, tells, if rightly understood, about this struggle. In the Epistle to Aristius Fuscus (I, 11) we read the fable of the stag and the horse who lost his liberty in order to eat better. In the Epistle *Quinque dies* (I, 7), Horace interprets his position by another fable. A fox penetrated through a small hole into a woven corn basket. He ate to his heart's content. And behold! The hole had become too narrow and he could not get out. Then the weasel gave him this advice: "If you want to get out, you must become as lean as you were when you went in." And Horace adds: "If that image concerns me, then I am prepared to resign everything. Then I will gladly praise the sleep of the poor not stuffed with fat capons, and I will not give up the leisure of liberty for all the riches of Arabia." These words are followed by the whimsically contemplative story of the great lord Philippus and the poor Volteius, who had been a junk dealer, as Horace's father once was. Once Philippus saw the poor Volteius sitting happily cleaning his fingernails with a knife in a barbershop, and he invited him to come for dinner. At first the poor man refuses. At last, however, he comes, and then comes more and more frequently. The fish swims toward the hook he does not see, says Horace. Philippus gives him an estate in the Sabine Hills, but he soon grows tired of it. Sheep are stolen from him. The goats die off. The fields do not flourish. Then he comes on his horse at night to his patron in the town and implores him: "Turn me back to my former life!" All that recalls, of course, Maecenas and Horace. One must understand that Horace would be ready to give back his Sabine estate to keep his liberty.

But how is this related to Horace as political poet? Were his political poems, his praises of Augustus, insincere flatteries? Were they written to order, propaganda, as Syme suggests in his book on the Roman revolution?[16] Were they something his heart was not in, as Wilkinson suggests?[17] There may be some truth in these statements. The Augustus Odes of the fourth book that praise the bringer of peace are written in the style of other encomia of rulers usual at the time, as we may conclude from inscriptions in Asia Minor. This *is* official poetry.

But first we must not forget that in spite of all the cruelties

---

[16] R. Syme, *The Roman Revolution* (Oxford, 1939), pp. 459 ff.
[17] Wilkinson, *Horace and His Lyric Poetry*, p. 65.

Octavian committed in connection with the civil war and after, struggling against conspiracies, the *Pax Augusta* and the renewal of order, justice, and religion in Rome were an achievement that was decisive for the further development and the stability of the Roman Empire. After endless wars and inexpressible cruelties the *Pax Augusta* seemed like a miracle. The history of the world changed. And then, being a Roman, Horace feels quite spontaneously responsible for the Roman State that was considered as something sacred, something beyond all discussion. Yet he was not blind to the faults of his age. He had the courage to speak with candor. That is proved by the *Roman Odes*, if they are rightly understood. They show a liberty and a depth of historical sense that must be admired.

In the first *Roman Ode* the ideal of poverty is praised. Poverty is considered as the thing to be sought in purposeful contrast to the life of the powerful and rich. The sorrows and fears of the mighty are pitilessly unmasked: You might have much land, you might boast glory and power, yet you must die, and fear and sorrow hang over you like the sword of Damocles and rob you of sleep. Thus the *Roman Odes*, strangely enough, begin with a poem that praises private existence and purposely depreciates political and social power. This ode (III, 1) is closely related to the ode we analyzed before (III, 29) that closes the third book. Thus the book is framed by personal confessions in an Epicurean spirit. Horace here describes his own personal ideal, but this ideal has a firm and necessary place in the system of Roman society. A political order that did not guarantee this private existence would have no value for Horace. For this reason the first *Roman Ode*, which praises this existence, has a firm place in the whole system of *Roman Odes* which are a symbol for the order of the total Roman existence. There is an ideal balance between the personal and the political realm, between individual and state, between Stoicism and Epicureanism. Both philosophies are necessary to give a theoretical basis to Roman life in its whole compass. This balance, which ascribes to both realms an independent and autonomous significance, is the great contribution that the Romans brought to Western civilization. For in Greece these two realms have the tendency to fall asunder. Either the polis or the individual is too mighty. And in the further course of our history this balance has been menaced time and again.

While the first *Roman Ode* remains in the private sphere of the poet, the second praises one of the most important social virtues: courage in military and political matters.

In the third *Roman Ode* too, a courageous and independent attitude is praised: the stoical Roman faithfulness to principle, especially to the central political virtue: justice and the courage to defend it against each menace. The *iustus et tenax propositi vir* who shows courage against the tyrant and the mass, who remains fearless even in the face of the end of the universe, *si fractus illabatur orbis impavidum ferient ruinae*, reminds us more of Cato than of Augustus. But in the next stanza Horace promises Augustus apotheosis on account of this very virtue. Horace seems to have wanted to pay homage to the adversaries of Augustus too, and making him in a way the heir of the Roman republic, commit him to the old Roman values. The legacy of the Republican fighters of Pharsalus and Philippi to whom Horace himself belonged is not to perish in the Augustan State. The ode has its climax in the speech of Juno, in which the condition of Roman greatness and Roman world rule is revealed: Troy has perished, but Rome, her heiress, will attain the empire of the world, if she condemns avarice (*aurum . . . spernere fortior*) and does not rebuild Troy. Otherwise the fate of Troy will be repeated. This is a very serious warning, for Troy is the city of injustice and greed.

The Fourth Ode displays in three ways the concept of *vis temperata*, the tempered power: in the poetry of Horace, in the peace of Augustus, and in the order of the world, that was made possible when the Olympians vanquished the Giants—the forces of destruction. Horace—Augustus—Jupiter: the poet—the Emperor—the god: these are the bearers of right order. The Muses give the advice of clemency: *vos lene consilium et datis et dato gaudetis . . .* , the poet, the "prophet of the Muses" (*Musarum sacerdos:* III, 1) can help the ruler to find the mild way to the right order. Here it becomes clear what Horace aims at: not so much the glorification of the Augustan order as the painting of a picture to which this order must conform.[18] It commits Augustus and the future emperors to the idea of justice and *vis temperata*. Horace becomes the defender

---

[18] The same is true of the speech of Jupiter in the first book of the *Aeneid*. It is much more than a praise of the *gens Julia*. It starts with Aeneas and ends with the Augustan order: the taming and subduing of the *Furor impius*, the self-destroying forces that brought about inexpressible sufferings.

of the order of state, proclaimed by Plato and Cicero. For the central ideas of this order are justice and moderation. Once again Augustan poetry takes over the heritage of Greek thought and Greek philosophy.

After this climax the Fifth and Sixth Odes are a kind of descent. In the Fifth Ode the decay of Roman virtue is described. This line is continued in the Sixth Ode, which paints the sexual demoralization in lurid colors. As a contrast appears the peasant youth of old Rome who worked the earth with a Sabellian mattock. The ode and the whole cycle end with a stanza full of deepest pessimism:

> "What do the ravages of time not injure! Our parents' age, worse than our ancestors', has brought forth us less worthy and destined soon to produce an offspring still more wicked."

> Damnosa quid non imminuit dies?
> aetas parentum, peior avis, tulit
> nos nequiores, mox daturos
> progeniem vitiosiorem.

The feeling of relentless decay intrudes with uncanny force. This dark end of the cycle is so amazing that commentators have passed it over with silence or have tried to explain it by a hypothesis of development in the poet, making the ode belong to a previous stage before the Augustan peace.[19] But I think we must recognize that this consciousness of guilt and sin and decay is one feature of the Augustan Age, too. The awareness that the Roman existence is menaced is not lacking even in the central *Roman Odes*, as is shown by the speech of Juno and the role of the Giants.

The peripheral Odes 1 and 6 treat the different expression of the Roman greed for life: the first *avaritia* and *luxuria* (avarice and luxurious living), the last the sexual demoralization. The Odes 2 and 5 correspond also: there the Homeric bravery of the lion-hearted hero, here the betrayal and the cowardice of a depraved generation. The central odes show the rescue, but also the danger: the Third Ode proclaims the Roman rule over the world and its conditions. The Fourth Ode shows the healing force of poetry and the benefit of the *Pax Augusta*. But this benefit can only abide when all are aware of the example the gods gave by the destruction of

---

[19] Cf. R. Heinze, *Vom Geist des Römertums* (Leipzig–Berlin, 1938), pp. 218 ff.

the wicked. So the most important motifs of Horatian poetry are encompassed in the *Roman Odes* as in a cone of light: hope of redemption and awareness of guilt; rescue and decay; the Epicurean salvation of the individual and the Roman virtue that proves itself in many aspects: as heroism in war, as contempt for the seducing goods of this world, as the subduing of the greed for life, and, not least, as the proud faithfulness to convictions that can if necessary defy political rulers. The poet is there, exhorting and helping, showing the way of salvation to the community. But if this way fails, if the forces of self-destruction go their way—and they will, so says the end of the Sixth Ode—then the individual still has a way to withdraw and to find a pleasant and peaceful happiness in the realm of the Muses and the natural joys of life. So Horace encompassed in these odes almost all aspects of his poetic mission, in a marvelously composed structure, written in the meter of the Greek poet Alcaeus. In this way he suggests that like Alcaeus, like the Greek poets of the early times, he unites political exhortation and the appeal to enjoy life wisely and cheerfully. He gathers the best forces of Greek poetry and philosophy and the best forces of Latinity. At the same time these poems grow out of an original and human personality, the poet Horace, who wants to achieve the personal life, this brief life that is given us here, to bring it to achievement through limitation. From such a poet, healing and beneficent forces can flow into our lives, too, if we listen to him.

George E. Duckworth

✧ THE "OLD" AND THE "NEW" IN VERGIL'S *AENEID*

Vergil ranks with Homer, Dante, and Milton as one of the supreme epic poets of Western literature, and, just as Vergil was indebted to Homer, so the achievements of the two later poets would have been impossible without the influence of the Roman poet. Vergil's pre-eminence was realized almost as soon as he began work on the *Aeneid;* the poet Propertius wrote (II, 34, 66): "Something greater than the *Iliad* is being born." A century after his death, as we learn from Martial (XIV, 186), expensive parchment editions of the epic were being produced as *Saturnalia* presents in late December; this was long before the Romans adopted Christianity, but it was a season of good will and a time for exchanging gifts.

Throughout the Roman Empire and the Middle Ages, Vergil was viewed as a source of all knowledge, as a teacher, a prophet, and even a magician.[1] Many of the medieval stories about his magical powers are fascinating and fantastic but, of course, they bear no relation to the true facts of his life. The real Vergil and his work emerge again with Dante, who loved him not only as a poet but as the one who had, in his Messianic Eclogue, bridged the gap between paganism and Christianity; hence it was Vergil whom Dante chose as his guide through Hell and Purgatory.[2] To Tenny-

---

[1] The best treatment of this aspect of Vergil is still D. Comparetti, *Virgil in the Middle Ages*, trans. E. F. M. Benecke (New York, 1929); see also J. W. Spargo, *Virgil the Necromancer* (Cambridge, Mass., 1934).

[2] See G. Highet, *The Classical Tradition* (New York, 1949), pp. 72–80.

son, Vergil was the "wielder of the stateliest measure ever moulded
by the lips of man,"[3] and T. S. Eliot calls him "the classic of all
Europe."[4] We should, I think, include the Americas and say that
he is "the classic of the western world."

The number of editions, books, and articles published each year
on Vergil's poetry is amazingly large. In recent years I have had
the pleasant, if somewhat laborious, task of preparing for the
Classical World two rather lengthy surveys of Vergilian bibliography.[5] I chose 1940 as my starting point because in that year an
Italian scholar named Mambelli published a two-volume bibliography of Vergil from 1900 on, and he listed almost 4,000 items—
an average of 100 a year.[6] This average has continued from 1940
to the present, as I discovered, somewhat unhappily, when I com-
piled my two bibliographical surveys.

How can we account for this tremendous output of new studies
on the poetry of Vergil? One reason, I believe, is that he differed
so strikingly from all previous poets and in every aspect of his work
created something new. The extent to which this statement is true
has been revealed only in recent decades. Earlier scholars were inclined to stress his borrowings from his predecessors, especially
Homer,[7] and we cannot deny that he made use of all earlier poetry,
both Greek and Roman. We find many deliberate echoes of En-
nius, Lucretius, and Catullus. Another great source of the *Aeneid*
is Greek tragedy, Euripides in particular,[8] and there seems a strong

---

[3] Highet, *ibid.*, p. 446, says of Tennyson: "He himself was surely the English Vergil;
and the address *To Vergil* which he wrote as a mature poet is among the finest tributes
ever paid by any artist to his predecessor."

[4] T. S. Eliot, *What Is A Classic?* (London, 1945), p. 31.

[5] G. E. Duckworth, "Recent Work on Vergil (1940–1956)," *C.W.* 51 (1957–58):
89–92, 116–17, 123–28, 151–59, 185–93, 228–35, reprinted in 1958 by the Vergilian
Society of America; "Recent Work on Vergil (1957–1963)," *C.W.* 57 (1963–64):
193–228, reprinted in 1964 by the Vergilian Society of America.

[6] G. Mambelli, *Gli studi virgiliani nel secolo XX: Contributo ad una bibliografia generale*
(Firenze, 1940).

[7] For the most complete study of Vergil's use of Homeric material, see G. N. Knauer,
Die Aeneis und Homer (Göttingen, 1964) [= *Hypomnemata*, Heft 7].

[8] See B. C. Fenik, *The Influence of Euripides on Vergil's "Aeneid"* (Ann Arbor, 1960)
[= Princeton University dissertation, microfilmed]. E. K. Rand, *The Magical Art of
Virgil* (Cambridge, Mass., 1931), p. 381, says: "the poem is not solely epic; in structure
it is a fusion of epic and of Attic tragedy, which Virgil enriches by creating a new
conception of fate."

probability that the range of his source material extended even to India, to the famous Sanskrit epic, the *Mahābhārata*.[9]

Today, however, thanks to the efforts of many twentieth-century scholars, we have a much clearer conception of Vergil's originality and the magnitude of his poetic achievement; in spite of his use of older material, the *Aeneid* is thoroughly Roman and thoroughly Vergilian, and it is new—new in content, in style, in poetic imagery, in use of language and meter, in its over-all structure. I shall examine briefly these various aspects of the poem.

Vergil is unlike any earlier poet, for he has produced a new kind of epic, with "a new vision of human nature and of heroic virtue";[10] it is a truly national epic, but it includes not only history (past, present, and future) but philosophy and religion as well. The characters are portrayed as individuals but they are also symbols and represent something outside of themselves and larger than themselves. As Pöschl says, "in Vergil the symbolic character of poetry is revealed with a clarity previously unknown in the history of Western poetic art."[11] In his recent and valuable book on Vergil, Otis attempts to explain how it was possible that "Virgil did what no one else had done before him and no one was able to do after him"; he was "the first and only poet truly to recreate the heroic-age epic in an urban civilization"; of all epic poetry "only the *Aeneid* aspired to be both heroic and civilized, both remote and contemporary, both Homeric and Augustan."[12]

Vergil's style is new; Otis calls it "subjective" as opposed to the more narrative, objective style of Homer and Apollonius; by "subjective" he means both the manner in which Vergil shares the emotions of his characters (empathy) and presents his own personal reaction to their emotions (sympathy). Otis writes: "Virgil not only reads the minds of his characters; he constantly communicates to us his own reactions to them and to their behaviour."[13] This "empathetic-sympathetic style" makes possible both a con-

---

[9] See G. E. Duckworth, "Turnus and Duryodhana," *T.A.P.A.*, 92 (1961): 81–127.

[10] C. M. Bowra, *From Virgil to Milton* (London, 1948), p. 35; see also pp. 10–15, 84–85.

[11] V. Pöschl, *The Art of Vergil: Image and Symbol in the "Aeneid,"* trans. G. Seligson (Ann Arbor, 1962), p. 1.

[12] B. Otis, *Virgil. A Study in Civilized Poetry* (Oxford, 1963), pp. 2–3.

[13] *Ibid.*, p. 88.

tinuous psychological narrative and the symbolic structure of the poem.

Vergil's poetic imagery differs from that of his predecessors; he takes over numerous similes from Homer and Apollonius, but he gives them another meaning and a new beauty. The similes are closely related to the inner struggles of the characters and often serve to forecast the fate in store for each. In IV, 441–46, we have the simile of the oak tree shakened by the northern winds; its leaves fall but it remains firm, its roots fast in the rocks; likewise Aeneas is buffeted by the entreaties of Anna, but (449):

> mens immota manet, lacrimae volvuntur inanes.

> "His resolve remains fixed, tears fall in vain."

Contrary to the statements in most commentaries on this passage, the tears here are those of Aeneas, for the simile expresses the inner conflict between his determination to depart and his love for Dido.[14] The comparison of Dido to a deer wounded by a shepherd (IV, 68–73) and that of Turnus to a wounded lion (XII, 4–9) not only reveal the state of mind of the two characters but provide a symbolic announcement of their later deaths.[15]

Vergil is painstaking in his use of language; each verse, each phrase, each word is significant, and the full meaning may come only with the second or third reading, and often there may be more than one meaning. The repetitions and echoes of words and phrases from earlier contexts serve to evoke symbolic associations. Alliteration had been a characteristic of Roman poetry from its very beginning, but Vergil is "the great master" of alliteration and expressiveness;[16] cf. I, 55 f. and 124:

> illi indignantes magno cum murmure montis
> circum claustra fremunt;

---

[14] See Pöschl (above, note 11), pp. 46 f.; G. E. Duckworth, *Structural Patterns and Proportions in Vergil's "Aeneid"* (Ann Arbor, 1962), p. 17, note 37. The English versions of the Latin passages given below are from the verse translation by L. R. Lind (Bloomington, 1962); Lind's translation of IV, 449, reproduces the wrong interpretation of *lacrimae inanes* ("his mind was unchanged. Vain tears rolled down Anna's cheeks.").

[15] Cf. Pöschl (above, note 11), pp. 79–81, 109–11.

[16] L. P. Wilkinson, *Golden Latin Artistry* (Cambridge, 1963), p. 85; cf. pp. 74–83 for his analysis of *Georgics* I, 43–392.

> interea magno misceri murmure pontum

> "Angry, they loudly protest against their confinement,
> The hill that lies over them.

> Meanwhile . . .
> The sea set roaring loudly in wild confusion."

In translation most of the original beauty is lost, and especially the effectiveness of the *m*-sounds. When the two serpents are described as coming from Tenedos to destroy Laocoon and his sons, the words hiss with sibilants, both initial and medial; cf. II, 207 ff.: *sanguineae superant undas, sinuatque immensa, sonitus spumante salo, ardentisque oculos suffecti sanguine.*

Vergil's meter often expresses the meaning of the sentence; the two most famous examples are undoubtedly VIII, 596, in which the horses gallop across the plain:

> quadripedante putrem sonitu quatit ungula campum.

> "Horses' hoofs
> with four-footed thud strike the crumbling field."

and VIII, 452, where the many spondees reproduce the sound of the Cyclopes working at their anvils:

> illi inter sese multa vi bracchia tollunt

> "Their great power
> Of arm lifted hammers."

The meter varies also in groups of lines and in episodes and speeches of considerable length. Vergil's most frequent combination of dactyls and spondees in the first four feet is *dsss;* this comprises about fourteen per cent of the *Aeneid* as a whole. The pattern occurs much more frequently, twenty to thirty per cent, in narrative episodes, such as battle descriptions, and especially in scenes of the gods and in passages dealing with Roman history and Augustus. In all such scenes a solemn and majestic rhythm is most appropriate. On the other hand, in the more dramatic and emotional episodes, those which best illustrate the new subjective

style, the frequency of *dss* varies usually from three to eight per
cent, far below the normal occurrence of this pattern. Meter, style,
and subject matter thus go hand in hand.[17] Another metrical innovation which we find in Vergil is a definite striving for variety.
The eight most frequent patterns, out of a possible sixteen, had
appeared in Lucretius 79.81 per cent of the total verses, and in
Catullus LXIV, the Peleus and Thetis poem, the frequency was
even higher, 90.98 per cent. Vergil reduced the frequency of his
first eight patterns in the *Aeneid* to 72.78 per cent.[18]

The *Aeneid* is one of the most consciously planned and carefully
constructed poems of world literature. Its architecture is most
unusual; we find not merely one structural pattern but at least
three.

First, there is an alternation of the books, those with even numbers being of a more serious and tragic nature than those with odd
numbers, which are lighter and serve to relieve tension. The famous
books which stand out in the reader's memory are even-numbered:
II, the fall of Troy; IV, the tragedy of Dido; VI, the trip to the
underworld; VIII, Aeneas' visit to Evander and the site of Rome;
X, the great battle, with the deaths of Pallas, Lausus, and Mezen-
tius; and XII, the final conflict and the death of Turnus. Vergil
has stressed the significance of these books by means of the alternating rhythm.

The *Aeneid* is divided into two halves, I–VI, often called the
"Odyssean" half of wanderings, and VII–XII, the "Iliadic" half
of battles after Aeneas and the Trojans arrive in Italy. Vergil himself looks upon the second half as a *maior rerum ordo*, a *maius opus*
(VII, 44 f.). The second architectural pattern is the parallelism,
by similarity and contrast, between the books in each half, I and
VII, II and VIII, III and IX, etc. For instance, in both I and VII
the Trojans arrive in a strange land and are welcomed after a
speech by the Trojan Ilioneus; in each the goddess Juno laments
her lack of power and stirs up trouble for the Trojans with divine

---

[17] See G. E. Duckworth, "Vergil's Subjective Style and Its Relation to Meter,"
Vergilius, 12 (1966): 1–10.

[18] The percentage of the first eight patterns in Vergil's *Eclogues* was 69.09; in the
Georgics 73.42. Horace surpassed Vergil in his desire for metrical variety: *Satires*, 69.99
per cent; *Epistles*, 66.76 per cent; see G. E. Duckworth, "Horace's Hexameters and
the Date of the *Ars Poetica*," *T.A.P.A.*, 96 (1965): 75 f., 92.

or infernal assistance—in I, the storm at sea, and in VII, the war in Latium.[19]

Vergil combines with the alternation of the books and their division into two corresponding halves a third and most important architectonic device—a tripartite division of the epic into three groups of four books each. The *Aeneid* gives not only the story of Trojan Aeneas but also the history of Rome and its destiny under Augustus. This latter provides much of the central core of the poem (V–VIII) and concludes with the victory of Augustus at Actium and his triumphs, described on the shield at the end of VIII. The *Aeneid* is thus a trilogy with the first four books, the tragedy of Dido, and the last four books, the tragedy of Turnus, enclosing and emphasizing the story of Rome and Augustus in the very center of the epic. This division of the poem into three parts is undoubtedly a deliberate attempt on Vergil's part to avoid too sharp a break into an "Odyssey" of wanderings and an "Iliad" of battles.[20]

I have discussed the structure of the *Aeneid* in some detail as it leads directly to my main theme—the "old" and the "new" in the *Aeneid* itself.

Of the even-numbered books the best known and best beloved is undoubtedly IV, which portrays the tragic love and suicide of Queen Dido of Carthage. Book VI is considered "the keystone of the whole poem," the "crowning Book, which Vergil has placed in the centre, to unite all that stand before it and all that stand after";[21] it tells how Aeneas, accompanied by the Sibyl and with

---

[19] For the similarities and contrasts in the corresponding books, see G. E. Duck-worth, "The Architecture of the *Aeneid*," *A.J.P.*, 75 (1954): 1–15, expanded in Duck-worth (above, note 14), pp. 7–10. Otis (above, note 12), pp. 217 f., 344 f., favors a different parallelism of the halves; he combines I and VII, but arranges the other books in reverse order: II and XII, III and XI, IV and X, V and IX, VI and VIII (see G. E. Duckworth, review of Otis in *A.J.P.*, 86 [1965]: 419 f.). Otis, however (pp. 392, 418), admits the validity of the correspondences in II and VIII, III and IX, etc.

[20] See G. E. Duckworth, "The *Aeneid* as a Trilogy," *T.A.P.A.*, 88 (1957): 1–10; (above, note 14), pp. 11–13.

[21] R. S. Conway, *Harvard Lectures on the Vergilian Age* (Cambridge, Mass., 1928), p. 143. Cf. also H. W. Prescott, *The Development of Virgil's Art* (Chicago, 1927), pp. 360 f.

the aid of the Golden Bough,[22] traverses both a "mythological" and a "philosophical" underworld, gains from his father Anchises an understanding of life and death, and learns of the future destiny of Rome; this book has recently been called "perhaps the most complex and poetically rich book of the poem."[23] On the other hand, Mackail says that Book XII, the final conflict of Aeneas and Turnus, "reaches an even higher point of artistic achievement and marks the utmost of what poetry can do, in its dramatic value, its masterly construction, and its faultless diction and rhythm."[24]

Two other books, likewise even-numbered and therefore of major significance, perhaps best present the basic theme of the *Aeneid;* these are II, the destruction of Troy, the end of the "old" city, and VIII, the rise of the "new" city, containing the description of early Rome and the scenes of Roman history on the shield. Vergil himself summarizes the two halves of the poem and its purpose in the opening verses (I, 1–7):

> arma virumque cano, Troiae qui primus ab oris
> Italiam fato profugus Lavinaque venit
> litora—multum ille et terris iactatus et alto
> vi superum, saevae memorem Iunonis ob iram,
> multa quoque et bello passus, dum conderet urbem
> inferretque deos Latio—genus unde Latinum
> Albanique patres atque altae moenia Romae.

> "I sing of arms and the man who first from Troy's shores,
> Fate's fugitive, came to Italy and Lavinium's
> Coast, a man much tossed on land and sea
> By the gods' force, through Juno's mindful fury;
> He suffered greatly in war until he could found
> A city and bring his gods to Latium, whence
> The Latins would spring, the Alban fathers, and Rome
> With its lofty walls."

The phrase, "to found a city and bring his gods to Latium," stresses both the political and the religious nature of the poem; Vergil adds in line 33:

---

[22] See R. A. Brooks, "*Discolor Aura*. Reflections on the Golden Bough," *A.J.P.*, 74 (1953): 260–80; C. P. Segal, "*Aeternum per saecula nomen*, the Golden Bough and the Tragedy of History," *Arion*, 4 (1965): 617–57; 5 (1966): 34–72.

[23] Segal, *Arion*, 5 (1966): 65.

[24] J. W. Mackail, "The *Aeneid* as a Work of Art," *C.J.*, 26 (1930–31): 17.

tantae molis erat Romanam condere gentem.

"So great
Was the task to found the race and the city of Rome."

Thus it is that Bowra considers the fundamental theme of the epic
to be "the destiny of Rome" as "presented in the person of Aeneas
who not only struggles and suffers for the Rome that is to be but
is already a typical Roman."[25] The miracle of the *Aeneid* is said to
be Vergil's ability to treat three different topics simultaneously—
the legendary narrative of Aeneas, themes and personages of
Roman history, and the praise of Augustus.[26] But, as I wrote some
years ago:[27]

> The epic rises far above the patriotic and historical level in the poet's
> dramatic treatment of character and event and in his introduction of
> loftier themes of philosophy and religion; it is an epic not only of Rome
> but of human life as well.

Perhaps nowhere in the *Aeneid* are the basic themes of the poem
displayed more clearly than in the two corresponding books, II
and VIII. Each, like the other books of the epic, is divided into
three main sections. In II we have (1) the stories of Sinon, Laocoon, and the wooden horse; (2) the return of the Greeks, the
capture of Troy, and the death of Priam; and (3) the Aeneas-
Venus episode, his return to his home, and the departure from
Troy, with the loss of Creusa. In VIII (1) Aeneas leaves the camp
of the Trojans and goes up the Tiber to Pallanteum, the site of
later Rome, where he is welcomed by King Evander and his son
Pallas; since a festival to Hercules is being celebrated, Evander describes the victory of Hercules over the monster Cacus; he then
leads Aeneas through the town, pointing out spots destined to be
famous later in the Roman city, and receives him in his humble
abode; (2) that night Venus persuades Vulcan to provide Aeneas
with armor, and early in the morning the god goes to his workshop
where the Cyclopes make the armor as instructed; (3) after Evan-

---

[25] Bowra (above, note 10), p. 36.

[26] See J. Perret, *Virgile, l'homme et l'oeuvre* (Paris, 1952), p. 89.

[27] G. E. Duckworth, "Mathematical Symmetry in Vergil's *Aeneid*," *T.A.P.A.*, 91
(1960): 185; (above, note 14), p. vii. J. W. Mackail, *Virgil and His Meaning to the
World of To-day* (New York, 1927), pp. 74–77, lists twelve aims which Vergil had in
mind while composing the *Aeneid*.

der's farewell to Pallas, the Trojans and their Arcadian allies set out for the Etruscan city of Caere and on the way Aeneas receives the armor from Venus; the book concludes with an account of the historical scenes on the shield. Such a brief summary, of course, fails to give an adequate conception of the power and richness of these two books or of Vergil's effective dramatic portrayal of Aeneas and the other characters.

In Books II and VIII, in addition to the fundamental contrast between the fall of the old city, characterized by darkness, despair, and death, and the rise of the new, accompanied by brightness, encouragement, and hope, other contrasts and similarities appear in abundance, as in the other pairs of corresponding books.[28] For example, in II the Greeks destroy Troy and the Trojans suffer at their hands, but in VIII the Greeks help to found Rome and the Trojans benefit from their assistance; the helplessness of the aged Priam in II is contrasted with the helpfulness of the aged Evander in VIII, as is the splendor of Priam's palace with the simplicity of Evander's home on the Palatine. Venus as a goddess appears to Aeneas in each book, in II to convince him that the gods favor the destruction of Troy, in VIII to present to him the armor, and on the shield the gods fight for Augustus and Rome at Actium against the barbarian deities of Antony and Cleopatra. In II Anchises is persuaded to leave Troy by a double prodigy—fire around the head of Ascanius and a comet in the sky; likewise, on the shield in VIII, fire appears around the temples of Augustus and over his head is his father's star, the comet of Julius Caesar. At the end of II Aeneas carries on his shoulders his father—a symbol of the past, and at the end of VIII he raises to his shoulder the shield portraying important scenes of Roman history—symbolic of the future. Aeneas marvels at the beauty of the shield but he is *rerum ignarus* (730); he does not realize the meaning of the scenes, unlike Vergil's contemporaries.

I should like to add two more pairs of passages to the similarities and contrasts already listed; both seem valid and significant.

1. In II the coming of the two serpents from Tenedos and the death of Laocoon and his sons are symbolic announcements of the

---

[28] See Duckworth, above, note 19.

return of the Greeks and the destruction of Troy,[29] and Hercules'
victory over Cacus in VIII, wrongly considered by some an episode contributing little to the action of the poem,[30] foreshadows
the final victory of Aeneas over Turnus, a necessary step to the
birth of Rome, and it also symbolizes the defeat of Antony and
Cleopatra by Augustus and the advent of peace in Vergil's own
day.[31] Otis looks upon the Hercules-Cacus story as "an example of
the conduct by which man can become divine and by which
Hercules himself became the true predecessor of Aeneas, Romulus
and Augustus."[32]

2. In II Aeneas first receives his commission; Hector appears
to him in a dream and urges him to flee with the Penates to a
new home across the seas; cf. 289–90, 293–95:

> "heu fuge, nate dea, teque his" ait "eripe flammis.
> hostis habet muros; ruit alto a culmine Troia. . . .
> sacra suosque tibi commendat Troia penatis;
> hos cape fatorum comites, his moenia quaere
> magna, pererrato statues quae denique ponto."

> "Run, goddess-born!" he said, "escape these flames:
> The enemy holds the walls; Troy-towers fall. . . .
>   Now she entrusts
> Her holy rites and statues to your care.

---

[29] See K. Büchner, *P. Vergilius Maro, Der Dichter der Römer* (Stuttgart, 1956) cols.
328 f. [= "Vergilius," *R.E.*, 16 (1958): cols. 1350 f.]; M. C. J. Putnam, *The Poetry
of the "Aeneid"* (Cambridge, Mass., 1965), p. 27. B. M. W. Knox, "The Serpent and
the Flame," *A.J.P.*, 71 (1950): 380, points out that the image of the serpent suggests
not only destruction but rebirth; "the death agonies of Troy are the birth-pangs of
Rome."

[30] See W. H. Semple, "The Conclusion of Virgil's *Aeneid*: A Study of the War in
Latium, with Special Reference to Books XI and XII," *B.R.L.*, 42 (1959–60): 180.
Semple (p. 181) lists the story of Nisus and Euryalus in IX as a similarly detached
episode which contributes nothing to the action of the plot or the progress of the war;
on this see G. E. Duckworth, "The Significance of Nisus and Euryalus for *Aeneid*
IX–XII," *A.J.P.*, 88 (1967): 129–50.

[31] See G. K. Galinsky, "The Hercules-Cacus Episode in *Aeneid* VIII," *A.J.P.*, 87
(1966): 18–51, and bibliography cited therein; cf. Duckworth, *C.W.*, 57 (1963–64):
209. Putnam (above, note 29), p. 35, compares also the forced entrance of Pyrrhus
into Priam's palace with Hercules' passage into the cave of Cacus and the revelation
of the interior of each (cf. the use of *apparere* in II, 483–84, and VIII, 241–42). The
serpent imagery, so prominent in II, is echoed in VIII; see Galinsky, *ibid.*, pp. 42 f.

[32] Otis (above, note 12), p. 335.

> Take them, the comrades of your fate, seek walls
> For them where they may rest, your wanderings over."

Aeneas ignores his duty; overcome by *furor* and *ira*, he rushes into battle in a vain attempt to save the doomed city from the Greeks; cf. 316–17:

> furor iraque mentem
> praecipitat, pulchrumque mori succurrit in armis.

> "Furious anger
> Drove me headlong, and all I thought was this:
> To die in battle is the way to glory."

Aeneas receives instructions and information concerning the future on many other occasions, from both gods and mortals: from Venus and Creusa in II; from Apollo, the Penates, Celaeno, and Helenus in III; from Mercury in IV; from Nautes and Anchises in V; and from the Sibyl in VI. Anchises, meeting Aeneas in the underworld, points out the souls to be reborn as Roman kings and heroes, including Augustus who is destined to bring to Rome a new Golden Age, and also describes the war to be waged by Aeneas in Latium and the toils to be undergone; cf. VI, 890–92:

> exim bella viro memorat quae deinde gerenda,
> Laurentisque docet populos urbemque Latini,
> et quo quemque modo fugiatque feratque laborem.

> "he told his hero-heir
> The wars which must be waged and described the peoples
> Of Laurentum, Latinus' city, and how he might flee
> From each trial, or bear it."

It is not until VIII 524–29, however, when Aeneas sees and hears the prodigy in the heavens—lightning, thunder, trumpet blasts, gleaming armor—that he realizes most fully that he is the divine man of Roman destiny. "I am summoned by Olympus" (*ego poscor Olympo*, 533),[33] he cries, and he foresees with sorrow the deaths and sufferings in store for the Latins and for Turnus. The *prodigium*, signifying that he will receive divine armor and engage

---

[33] I follow here the punctuation of Sabbadini and most other editors; Hirtzel (Oxford Classical Text) joins *Olympo* to the following sentence.

in war, brings to a close the long series of warnings and instructions which began with the words of Hector in II. This time Aeneas shows no hesitation and accepts willingly the difficult duties which lie ahead. It is thus in VIII that Aeneas becomes a truly religious hero, endowed with the spiritual energy necessary for his destined task.[34]

One important feature of Book II is Vergil's emphasis on the bravery of the Trojans and Aeneas. They were the equal of the Greeks in battle, and it was only by trickery and the will of the gods that they were defeated; cf. 195–98:

> Talibus insidiis periurique arte Sinonis
> credita res, captique dolis lacrimisque coactis
> quos neque Tydides nec Larisaeus Achilles,
> non anni domuere decem, non mille carinae.[35]

> "With such deceits and wicked art of Sinon,
> By tricks and tears, the captive made us believe him,
> We whom no Achilles of Larissa nor Diomedes
> Nor ten years nor a thousand ships had conquered."

and the words of Venus in 601–3:

> "non tibi Tyndaridis facies invisa Lacaenae
> culpatusve Paris, divum inclementia, divum,
> has evertit opes sternitque a culmine Troiam."

> "Do not blame the hated beauty of Helen, nor Paris:
> The merciless gods, the gods, are the ones who have toppled
> The power of Troy and levelled it with the earth."

The Trojans and Aeneas must appear as worthy ancestors of the Romans. Aeneas therefore ignores the instructions of Hector and rushes blindly with his companions to the defense of the city. Father Sullivan says:[36]

---

[34] See F. A. Sullivan, S.J., "The Spiritual Itinerary of Virgil's Aeneas," *A.J.P.*, 80 (1959): 150–61. F. Bömer, "Studien zum VIII. Buche der Aeneis," *R.M.*, 92 (1944): 319–69, discusses the structural importance of the prodigy-episode (520–40) for the unity of VIII and calls it the "Höhepunkt" of the book; cf. pp. 322, 326, 337, 340.

[35] The repetition of the words *dolus* and *insidiae* is especially effective; in addition to 195 and 196, cf. *dolo* (34), *dolis Danaum* (44), *dolos* (62), *dolis et arte Pelasga* (152), *Myrmidonumque dolos* (252), *doli fabricator* (264); *Danaum insidias* (36, 65), *Danaum . . . insidiae* (309 f.).

[36] Sullivan (above, note 34), pp. 152–53.

His *pietas* towards the gods seems eclipsed by *furor;* his *pietas* towards his family is forgotten, and only for his *patria*, now doomed and in flames, does he show any thought. . . . Blind *furor* must give way to a new faith, despair to a new hope before he can become a vessel of election for the great task ahead.

It is in VI and finally in VIII that Aeneas gains the faith and hope which carry him through the difficult days of the fighting in the latter portion of the epic.

I return now to Book VIII, which is perhaps less familiar than II to many lovers of Vergil. After the cruel death of Priam and the destruction of Troy, it comes somewhat as a surprise to find Greeks and Trojans joining in a treaty of friendship. The Sibyl, however, in her pessimistic and enigmatic prophecy, had said (VI, 96–97):

"via prima salutis,
quod minime reris, Graia pandetur ab urbe."

"The first road to safety will open
From a Greek city, where you would least expect it."

There are several reasons for the union of the Arcadian Greeks of Pallanteum and the Trojans, as we learn from the speeches of Aeneas (127–51) and Evander (154–74): the two peoples have a common ancestry from Atlas and they have a common enemy, the Rutulians; they are bound by guest friendship, for Priam and Anchises had once visited Arcadia and Anchises had presented gifts to Evander, then a mere youth. Furthermore, Evander and the Arcadians, like Aeneas and the Trojans, were exiles from their home and had been led to Italy by Fate and Apollo (cf. 333–36).

It was a stroke of genius on the part of Vergil to have Aeneas leave the Trojan camp and visit Evander at the site of Rome. The values of the Evander episode and its effects on the latter part of the *Aeneid* are numerous and far-reaching, and may be enumerated briefly as follows:

1. Structurally, Aeneas' absence from the Trojan camp, like Achilles' refusal to fight in the *Iliad*, gives the enemy an opportunity to play a leading role; this results in the activity of Turnus in Book IX and the fight within the Trojan camp. Aeneas' absence likewise gives Ascanius a chance to display qualities of leadership

and provides motivation for the ill-fated night expedition of Nisus and Euryalus.

2. The numerous leaders and warriors catalogued in VII, 641–817, join the Latins and Rutulians; the Trojans, unless they are to be hopelessly outnumbered, are in desperate need of allies, and Evander not only provides Greek warriors but sends him to the leaderless Etruscans who will add thousands of fighters to the Trojan side. The war now ceases to be a local skirmish and becomes a major conflict involving all of central and northern Italy, even beyond the river Po, as far north as Mantua, Vergil's birthplace (cf. X, 198–206). The fact that Vergil has given Greek ancestry and Greek connections to so many warriors in the catalogue in VII tends to make the ensuing conflict almost a continuation on Italian soil of the Greco-Trojan War.[37]

3. Pallas, Evander's youthful son, who accompanies Aeneas into battle, is a key figure in the later action; Turnus' insolent words and actions when he slays Pallas in X (cf. *iussa superba*, 445; *superbum caede nova*, 514 f.) are directly responsible for his own death at the end of XII;[38] Aeneas was about to spare Turnus when he saw the sword-belt of Pallas and cried out (947–49):

> "tune hinc spoliis indute meorum
> eripiare mihi? Pallas te hoc vulnere, Pallas
> immolat et poenam scelerato ex sanguine sumit."

> "Shall you escape me with spoils you have taken
> From those I have loved? Pallas with this wound shall
> slay you
> In sacrifice, Pallas exacts from your villainous blood
> His penalty!"

4. Aeneas' visit to Evander explains the presence of a Greek cult in Roman religion—the cult of Hercules at the *ara maxima* in

---

[37] Cf. VII, 656 (*satus Hercule*), 672 (*Argiva iuventus*), 679 (*Volcano genitum*), 691 (*Neptunia proles*), 723 (*Agamemnonius, Troiani nominis hostis*), 761 (*Hippolyti proles*), 794 (*Argivaque pubes*). See A. Cartault, *L'art de Virgile dans l'Énéide* (Paris, 1926), pp. 560–62.

[38] See G. E. Duckworth, "Fate and Free Will in Vergil's *Aeneid*," *C.J.*, 51 (1955–56): 362; R. Hornsby, "The Armor of the Slain," *Philol. Quart.*, 45 (1966): 357–59. Putnam (above, note 29), pp. 151–52, 189, 192, presents a picture of Aeneas' force and violence at the end of XII which many will find unacceptable. I do not agree with Putnam (p. 193) that Aeneas, in slaying Turnus, disregards Anchises' words in VI, 853; *debellare superbos* is his duty.

the Forum Boarium; this religious rite goes back to early times, before the foundation of Rome. Evander explains the cult as the result of their gratitude to Hercules for destroying Cacus.[39]

5. The union of Greek and Trojan forces in VIII symbolizes the later incorporation of Greek influences in the Roman State. The culture of Vergil's day was as much Greek as Roman. Likewise, the influence of the Etruscans on Roman architecture, government, and religion had been far from inconsiderable, and this too is symbolized by the union of Trojan and Etruscan forces in the *Aeneid*.

6. Aeneas' visit to the site of Rome provides a strong patriotic and antiquarian interest. One always wishes to know about the early days of one's home town or home city. Less than a hundred years ago the present Lincoln Center in New York City was farmland, from which people moved into the city, as it was too far away for commuting; the Public Library at the corner of Fifth Avenue and Forty-Second Street was a goat pasture. Romans of Vergil's day likewise would be fascinated by the description of the Forum as a cow pasture, and of the Capitoline as merely a grove where the presence of a god, perhaps Jupiter, was felt. The contrast between this early period and the splendor of the city in the time of Augustus would make a strong appeal to the pride of Vergil's readers.

Aeneas visits the very heart of Rome, the Capitoline,[40] Forum, and Palatine—the religious, political, business, and residential centers of the later city. But Vergil not only describes an imaginary primitive settlement of the past; at the same time he recalls the topographical present, certain monuments erected in his own day:

[39] The cult was not entirely Greek, however, but contained Italian elements; cf. Galinsky (above, note 31), p. 46.

[40] Cf. 347: *hinc ad Tarpeiam sedem et Capitolia ducit.* W. W. Fowler, *Aeneas at the Site of Rome* (Oxford, 1918), p. 73, suggests that Evander and Aeneas stopped at "the foot of the Capitol"; at this spot it would be impossible to see the *arx* (357); moreover, in order to point out the Lupercal on the right, the asylum on the left, and the Argiletum straight ahead, Evander had already led Aeneas past the Tarpeian rock; why should they retrace their steps? The verb *ducit* (347) is in sharp contrast to *monstrat* (337, 343, 345); it seems more likely, therefore, that Evander, in spite of his age (*obsitus aevo*, 307) took Aeneas up the Capitoline hill (by way of the later *clivus Capitolinus*) from which they could gain a better view of both the Janiculum and the *arx;* cf. Cartault (above, note 37), p. 609; Rand (above, note 8), p. 427, who says: "And now they climb the Capitoline."

porta Carmentalis (338) was adjacent to the later temple of Apollo, and both the temple and the Lupercal (343) had been restored by Augustus; the grove of Argiletum (345) suggests the Basilica Aemilia and the Curia, both completed by Augustus, and perhaps also the Gates of Janus nearby, which the *princeps* had closed after so long a period of civil conflict (cf. I, 293–96); the description of the Capitoline and the presence of Jupiter is probably a reference, not to the great temple of Jupiter, Juno, and Minerva, but to a smaller temple on the Capitoline to *Jupiter Tonans*, dedicated by Augustus in 22 b.c.[41]

However, in spite of these possible allusions to his own day, Vergil actually presents the setting, the "empty stage," for the later history of the city. For the events to take place on this historic site, we turn to the scenes on the shield of Aeneas at the end of the book, beginning with Romulus and Remus and ending with Augustus.[42] The scenes include the rape of the Sabine women and the later union of Sabines and Latins; the punishment of Mettus for his treachery; the fight with the Etruscans and Horatius at the bridge; Manlius defending the Capitoline against the Gauls; Catiline and Cato; and in the center of the shield (*in medio*, 675),[43] Augustus' victory over Antony and Cleopatra at Actium and his triple triumph.

Many have asked why Vergil chose these particular scenes. What is their underlying unity, if any? The poet himself describes the shield in 626, 628–29 as containing:

[41] See P. Grimal, "La promenade d'Évandre et d'Énée à la lumière des fouilles récentes," *R.E.A.*, 50 (1948): 348–51; cf. Galinsky (above, note 31), p. 21. On the temple of Jupiter Tonans, cf. also Cartault (above, note 37), p. 609; Bömer (above, note 34), p. 326.

[42] Cf. the juxtaposition of Romulus and Augustus in I, 272–96, and VI, 777–807. Suetonius (*Divus Augustus*, 7) relates that some senators had preferred the title "Romulus" to "Augustus" as more suitable for the second founder of Rome.

[43] Fowler (above, note 40), pp. 100 f., thinks it futile to attempt to locate the scenes on the shield; so Otis (above, note 12), p. 341: the shield "is assuredly *not* to be reduced to any one plan that can be visualized." But Vergil apparently did intend us to think of the arrangement of the scenes; cf. *in summo* (652), *haec inter* (671), *in medio* (675); see Cartault (above, note 37), pp. 622–32, who places the scenes clockwise in a series of outer and inner panels or compartments. Cf. also *The Works of Virgil*, translated by C. Pitt, with Notes by J. Warton (London, 1763), III; the scenes on the reproduction facing p. 321 go counterclockwise; see W. Whitehead, "Observations on the Shield of Aeneas," *ibid.*, pp. 340–52.

res Italas Romanorumque triumphos . . .
genus omne futurae
stirpis ab Ascanio pugnataque in ordine bella.

"Italian history, triumphs
Of Romans, the people that were to descend from Ascanius,
The wars they would fight, each in order."

Fowler suggests that the scenes are all "escapes from terrible perils,"[44] and Otis considers the main theme of the shield to be "the constant opposition of *virtus, consilium* and *pietas* to the forces of violence in all Roman history."[45] I prefer to find the unity of the shield elsewhere. The events described from early Roman history all took place in or near Rome itself, and, after the battle of Actium (675–713), we return to Rome for the triumphs of Augustus and the survey of the conquered nations (714–28). We thus have in VIII a dramatic progression from Evander's primitive settlement, the empty stage, to the shield on which the events to take place at Rome are described, those both of its early history and of Vergil's own day.[46] This completes the rise of the new city in VIII and balances the fall of the old in II. Aeneas lifts to his shoulder a picture of Rome's history and Rome's destiny.

Book II, the destruction of Troy, is one of the great books of the *Aeneid*, but structurally it does not have the significance of VIII, the final book of the central third of the poem.[47] In this respect, VIII is to be compared with IV, the Dido book, and XII, the Turnus book. Each is the conclusion of one section of the trilogy, and the central, more Roman and Augustan portion, reaches a fitting climax in the picture of Rome, its early history, and the battle of Actium which makes possible the Augustan Age—the return of the *aurea saecula*.

[44] Fowler (above, note 40), pp. 103–6; he is troubled by the fact that the greatest escape of all, that from Hannibal and Carthaginian domination, is omitted. However, if we reject Fowler's theory of "great escapes" in favor of "events at Rome," the omission of Hannibal presents no problem; Rome itself was not attacked by Carthaginian forces, as by the Gauls a century and a half earlier. And, in any case, Vergil has stressed the hostility of Rome and Carthage elsewhere in the *Aeneid*; cf. I, 12–22; IV, 622–29; X, 11–14.

[45] Otis (above, note 12), p. 341; cf. Putnam (above, note 29), p. 150: "And this is the story of the shield—violence ultimately leading to peace."

[46] Cf. Cartault (above, note 37), p. 634; Otis (above, note 12), p. 342.

[47] Otis (above, note 12), pp. 273 f., 343–45, 419, adds IX to the four central books; this destroys the climactic effect of the conclusion of VIII and blurs the relation of the Nisus-Euryalus episode to the remainder of the epic; see Duckworth (above, note 30), pp. 141–47.

Wolfgang Clemen

❧ THE UNIQUENESS OF SPENSER'S *EPITHALAMION*

Spenser's *Epithalamion* is one of the great poems of English literature. It has maintained its reputation and rank throughout the centuries in spite of the changes in taste and outlook.[1] In reading it today we can still enjoy it with that immediacy of pleasure which also for a closer scholarly investigation forms the best condition. We can still appreciate the beautiful melody of the stanzas, the imaginative richness of the language, the freshness of the poem and its personal tone, the intensity of emotion, the moving union of the sensuous and the spiritual, the striking fusion of many disparate elements; we can still enjoy the dramatic presentation of scene and action, the wealth of visual and oral impressions, the vividness of concrete details.

There are only a few random impressions which the ordinary, unprepared reader might share with us, but despite their value as an indication of the poem's enduring effect, they are too vague and general for a discriminating evaluation. The scholar is constantly faced with the task of penetrating to the core of impressions such as these, and, by tracing each one back to its component aspects, he may transform a mere impression into demonstrable fact. The effect of artistic perfection and emotional intensity, the impression of what we would call high poetic quality, is usually a product of a number of factors co-operating toward a common goal.[2] In read-

[1] For assessments see *The Works of Edmund Spenser. A Variorum Edition, The Minor Poems*, II (Baltimore, 1947).

[2] Cf. René Wellek, *Concepts of Criticism* (New Haven, 1963).

ing a poem only one or twice we cannot become aware of this complicated interplay of various elements. It is only by closer examination that we discover how many different things had to come together to make this achievement possible.

Moreover, a poem of great perfection and great beauty often forms a milestone in the history of English poetry. Its freshness and liveliness derive from the fact that certain structural qualities, certain principles of composition and poetic organization, were achieved here for the first time in a successful manner. The poet who writes a perfect poem that may be regarded as a climax in the poetry of his time has usually succeeded in solving problems for which neither his predecessors nor even he himself in earlier poems had managed to find a satisfactory solution. Poetry, in spite of its claim to inspiration, is an art in which much has to be learned before a masterpiece can be produced. The instruments of versification and diction must be refined to a degree of perfection, devices of composition and organization must have been found, means of poetic expression must have been developed, ways of giving shape to abstract notions must be at the poet's disposal in order that a successful "long poem" of some complexity may be born.

Looking back over the history of English poetry in the sixteenth century, and examining the way in which these arts of poetic composition and expression developed, we would have to admit that the *Epithalamion* could not have been written in the sixties, seventies or eighties of the sixteenth century. A process of gradual development was necessary for English poetry to reach a stage at which a man of genius like Spenser could find at his disposal an instrument sufficiently refined to enable him to write a great poem. This does not mean that the evolution of a style of poetry over a period of several decades would automatically lead to a masterpiece. However, it was not mere chance that Spenser's achievement with his *Epithalamion* appeared at the same time as the crowning achievement of Elizabethan lyric poetry, as a consummation of some of the highest potentialities and poetic endeavors of this important phase in English poetry. It is with a view to this twofold quality of Spenser's *Epithalamion*, as a great representative poem of the English Renaissance and as Spenser's most perfect work of art, that I propose to speak of its "uniqueness."

"Uniqueness" and "perfection," however, are the results of the fortunate co-operation of several basic qualities. I should like therefore to concentrate on the question: What are the distinguishing features which go to constitute the poem's excellence and its uniqueness? It may be appropriate to gauge these qualities first by looking back on works of comparable length and subject matter written before Spenser's poem.

Spenser's *Epithalamion* is one of these "long poems" which in the literature of the sixteenth century form a class of their own. A "long poem" has always set special problems for its author.[3] It has a tendency to become tedious, so variety, change in tone and color, but also growth and development, are essential. But this again might well impair the poem's unity and consistency. Thus the special difficulties attributed to the long poem have often been the problems of organization and of unification. And we can easily see that the long poems before Spenser generally fail in this respect.[4] They could just as well go on for another ten stanzas, they have no climax and often no central theme to which all minor details should be related. They are loosely constructed and their method of composition is rather one of stringing together a series of ideas, conventions, and incidents. The Epithalamies[5] by Bartholomew Young and Sir Philip Sidney are particularly suited for such a comparison as they belong to the same literary genre and employ similar conventions to Spenser's *Epithalamion*. In Young's *Epithalamion*, for instance, the sequence of the stanzas could even be changed without detriment to the intelligibility of the poem; there is no link between the stanzas and little or no connection between the different motifs which are treated separately in the course of the poem. Spenser's poem, on the other hand, displays unity, order, inner cohesion, and clear organization. In fact, it appears to be the first long poem in the history of English poetry to be composed according to a well-calculated plan. It has its own curve and development, its proper preparation at the beginning leading us leisurely and step by step toward the core of the poem and it has

---

[3] On this aspect, in view of Spenser's achievement, see W. H. Stevenson, "The Spaciousness of Spenser's 'Epithalamion,' " *R.E.L.*, 5 (1964): 61–69.

[4] E. G. Daniel's "The Complaint of Rosamond," Ralegh's "Cynthia," Barnfield's "The Affectionate Shepheard."

[5] Reprinted in Robert H. Case, *English Epithalamies* (London, 1896).

its proper ending. We can even detect an elaborate symmetry, so characteristic of Renaissance art, in the construction of this poem.

After the invocation to the Muses ten stanzas out of twenty-three lead up to the great moment when the bride enters the church, so that the actual marriage ceremony takes place in the exact center of the poem. But this marriage ceremony also coincides with the middle of the day, with the sun reaching its zenith. Two structural patterns thus correspond to each other, and the two halves into which we can divide the poem (if we take the middle of the day with the wedding ceremony as the division line) also bear resemblances to each other and disclose correspondences. Thus, as William Nelson has pointed out in his recent book on Spenser[6] "the opening invocation of the Muses, the Nymphs, the Hours and the Graces is matched by concluding prayers to Cynthia, Juno, Genius, Hebe and the 'high heavens.' The bride is roused from sleep at the beginning and is sung to sleep at the end. The rising sun has its balance in the evening star, the moon, and the 'thousand torches flaming bright.' In the morning the Hours are asked to adorn and array the bride; when the sun sets the attendant damsels disarray her." Another critic, Hieatt, has gone even further and has tried to point out, as regards the use of numbers and recurring motifs, subtle correspondences between the stanzas occupying the same position in both parts.[7]

As Spenser describes the progress of his marriage day from early morning until late at night, his poem is given a definite framework of time and experience. But within this running action each stanza depicts a situation, a moment or a phase which is complete in itself and forms a unit within the larger composition of the whole poem. This art of elaborating a situation, presenting it to us as a living picture but integrating this pictorial mode of presentation into a steadily progressing action, is evident in Spenser's *Faerie Queene*. In the *Epithalamion* this art reappears in a more concentrated form combined with a convincing and well-rounded cyclic pattern. For the natural order of a twenty-four-hour cycle binds the happenings of the poem close together and also places the

---

[6] William Nelson, *The Poetry of Edmund Spenser* (New York, 1963), p. 95.

[7] A. Kent Hieatt, *Short Time's Endless Monument. The Symbolism of the Numbers in Edmund Spenser's* Epithalamion (New York, 1960).

reader in a revolving time scheme which he may relate to his own daily experience. The order and ritual of the marriage day in accordance with the custom of the time are carefully observed; the progress of the marriage procession bringing the bride from her home to the church and taking her back to her home constitutes a conspicuous groundplan and allows every minor detail as well as every convention of the epithalamic tradition to fall into its concrete place in time and locality. For when reading the poem we always know where and in which phase of the day we find ourselves. Thus we can say that in Spenser's poem order and organization are closely combined with a constant endeavor to relate all traditional conventions and motifs to the specific happenings of this marriage day; a process which we might call "concretization."

However, order and organization in a perfect poem are inevitably linked with the problem of unity. Unity is not uniformity. For uniformity effected through monotonous versification and diction, the regular recurrence of certain rhetorical figures or conventions was what the poets before Spenser had as a rule produced instead of genuine unity. Spenser's poem, however, is a work of variety, of changing tempo and diction, of surprising transitions between varying levels of style and techniques of description. To give unity to such a poem of many colors and great diversity, Spenser had to use several means. (Whether the poet contrived these means consciously or unconsciously is a problem which we cannot discuss here.) However, we could draw up a long list of features and devices which contribute toward unifying of the poem. I can mention here only a few.

In several respects the bride is the center of the poem, the pervading theme to which everything else is related. To begin with, Spenser succeeds in connecting most of the minor decorative details, almost all the ornament and imagery, with the bride, who is referred to in almost every stanza. The nymphs, the graces, and the village girls are invoked to awaken, to adorn, to dress the bride; to sing her praise, to help in the preparation of the wedding. But the same applies to others appearing in the course of the poem—the "fresh boyes" (112), the minstrels, the damsels in the street, the virgins, and also the non-human beings—the birds, the woods, the moon, the evening-star, the night, the "sonnes of Venus." This unifying effect, if we may put it that way, is enhanced by the fact that it is the poet himself who calls upon all these beings and people to serve the bride in some way or other, to sing her praise, to contribute to her happiness and well-being.

The poet is at the same time the bridegroom, who describes his own marriage day and gives his entire poem as a present to his bride. But his role is also that of a director of a masque or pageant, for, like a master of the revels, he arranges everything and the main initiative always comes from him. He is also the speaker who in his complex role as poet, bridegroom, and master of the revels can address his own bride with the same naturalness as the Muses, Juno, or the "merchants daughters." This continuous presence of the poet himself, acting beside the bride as the second central figure in the poem and to whose voice we listen, not only increases the personal meaning and appeal of this poem but is another important factor in producing its unity. Moreover, the poem in itself appears as a gift from the poet to his bride, as an "ornament" that crowns the activity of adorning and praising referred to in every stanza. The poem's last stanza, the "envoy," reads:

> Song made in lieu of many ornaments,
> With which my love should duly have bene dect,

ending

> Be unto her a goodly ornament,
> And for short time an endlesse moniment.[8]

Now we find that this motif of adorning is one of the recurring leitmotifs. The Muses often helped the poets "others to adorne" (2). The whole third stanza is about the adorning of the bridal chambers, and in the fourth stanza it is the bride herself who is to be adorned. In the sixth stanza the three Graces are called upon to "adorne my beautifullest bride" (105). I quote the third stanza to illustrate the manner in which Spenser interweaves this motif of adorning into the running account of the marriage day:

> Bring with you all the Nymphes that you can heare
> Both of the rivers and the forrests greene:
> And of the sea that neighbours to her neare,
> Al with gay girlands goodly wel beseene.

---

[8] The text used is that of the Variorum Edition of *The Works of Edmund Spenser* (Baltimore, 1947). The letters u-v, and i-j have, however, been modernized.

And let them also with them bring in hand
Another gay girland
For my fayre love of lillyes and of roses,
Bound truelove wize with a blew silke riband.
And let them make great store of bridale poses,
And let them eeke bring store of other flowers
To deck the bridal bowers.
And let the ground whereas her foot shall tread,
For feare the stones her tender foot should wrong
Be strewed with fragrant flowers all along,
And diapred lyke the discolored mead.
Which done, doe at her chamber dore awayt,
For she will waken strayt,
The whiles doe ye this song unto her sing,
The woods shall to you answer and your Eccho ring.

Singing and *rejoicing* are other often recurring motifs which help to convey a certain coloring and mood to this poem. Or note the frequency of words expressing joy: *joyance, pleasure, pleasance, delight, happiness, jollity, cheerful, glad, happy,* or the frequency of other key words like *fair, fresh, sweet, goodly, gentle, seemly.*

Such a use of vocabulary may also be found in other Elizabethan poems. But of a more intricate and subtle effect as a unifying factor is the imagery of light which pervades the whole poem. For it is derived quite organically from the rising and descending sun, followed by the rising moon. These metaphors of light, however, are invariably related to the bride, so that there is a constant fluctuation and correspondence between the real sun and its symbolic significance. The seventh stanza may illustrate this point:

Now is my love all ready forth to come,
Let all the virgins therefore well awayt,
And ye fresh boyes that tend upon her groome
Prepare your selves; for he is comming strayt.
Set all your things in seemely good aray
Fit for so joyful day,
The joyfulst day that ever sunne did see.
Faire Sun, shew forth thy favourable ray,
And let thy lifull heat not fervent be
For feare of burning her sunshyny face,
Her beauty to disgrace.

O fayrest Phœbus, father of the Muse,
If ever I did honour thee aright,
Or sing the thing, that mote thy mind delight,
Doe not thy servants simple boone refuse,
But let this day let this one day be myne,
Let all the rest be thine.
Then I thy soverayne prayses loud wil sing,
That all the woods shal answer and theyr eccho ring.

Thus we find that the organization of unity is closely bound up with the establishing of correspondences and interrelationships. The course of outward events, the situations visually described, and the stages of this marriage day are at the same time, as a more detailed study might show, expressive of inner moods. The outward form of this poem has become "inner form," for the curve of external happenings on this marriage day coincides with the curve of inner experience. The day's natural cycle governed by the rising and setting sun is a perfect image of what the poet wanted to convey in the sphere of ideas, feelings, and ethical values.

But unity also means integration of heterogeneous elements. Let us begin with the integration of the traditional conventions which belonged to the "epithalamium." The apparatus of epithalamic conventions has been carefully explored by several scholars.[9] Spenser observes most of these conventions but we are scarcely aware of their "conventional origin," for he has enlivened and concretized them by relating them closely to the actual events of the day and by turning them to dramatic account. Even the first invocations to the nymphs and the graces (37, 103) are utilized in this particular manner. The nymphs, for example, are called upon to decorate the bridal bowers with flowers and to wait for the bride at the chamber door, thus resembling the customary bridesmaids who appear at a wedding (45 ff.). But if we read on we notice that the "light foot maids" (67) who are addressed as the "Nymphes of Mulla" are more or less identical with the daughters of the tenants and farmers in the country round the castle of Kilcolman where Spenser's marriage actually took place. In other

---

[9] Thomas M. Greene, "Spenser and the Epithalamic Convention," *Comparative Literature*, 9 (1957): 215–28. Hallett Smith, "The Use of Conventions in Spenser's Minor Poems," *Form and Convention in the Poetry of Edmund Spenser, English Institute Essays* (New York, 1961), pp. 122–45.

stanzas, too, the mythological figures merge into the familiar people of Spenser's own countryside, just as the ideal scenery and the conventional setting of the *Epithalamion* constantly blend with the local Irish scenery and the actual circumstances of Spenser's marriage day.[10] Mythology, on the other hand, is fused with folk-lore and popular custom, so that there is a constant transition between the literary tradition of the "epithalamium" and the actual wedding customs still in use in Spenser's own time. This point may be illustrated by the stanzas VIII (129 ff.) or XV (260 ff.) where we hear of the festivities connected with St. Barnabas Day, or stanza XIX (334 ff.), where there is mention of "Pouke" and "other evill sprights" and "mischivous witches with theyr charmes." The stanza should be quoted in full:

> Let no lamenting cryes, nor dolefull teares,
> Be heard all night within nor yet without:
> Ne let false whispers breeding hidden feares,
> Breake gentle sleepe with misconceived dout.
> Let no deluding dreames, nor dreadful sights
> Make sudden sad affrights;
> Ne let housefyres, nor lightnings helpelesse harmes,
> Ne let the Pouke, nor other evill sprights,
> Ne let mischivous witches with theyr charmes,
> Ne let hob Goblins, names whose sence we see not,
> Fray us with things that be not.
> Let not the shriech Oule, nor the Storke be heard:
> Nor the night Raven that still deadly yels,
> Nor damned ghosts cald up with mighty spels,
> Nor griesly vultures make us once affeard:
> Ne let th'unpleasant Quyre of Frogs still croking
> Make us to wish theyr choking.
> Let none of these theyr drery accents sing;
> Ne let the woods them answer, nor theyr eccho ring.

If we listen to a reading of Spenser's *Epithalamion* we become particularly aware of the unifying function of the refrain at the end of each stanza. This most musical and perfect refrain not only

---

[10] Thus in the fourth stanza Spenser evokes the scenery round his castle in referring to the "silver scaly trouts" on which Renwick (in his edition of the *Epithalamion*) remarks: "There are good trout in Awbeg still." (*Daphnaïda and other Poems*, ed. by W. L. Renwick [London, 1929], p. 205.)

rounds off each stanza but also evokes the same symbolic background of scenery and echoing music to which the stanza contributes its own particular feature. However, this refrain is more than a recurring leitmotif. For through the slight modification to which each new refrain is submitted we are reminded of the gradual passage of time. Whereas the sixteenth stanza describing the last part of the day ended "That all the woods them answer and their echo ring" the following stanza (the seventeenth) emphasizes the beginning of night with lines like:

> Now day is doen, and night is nighing fast:
> Now bring the Bryde into the brydall boures.
> Now night is come, now soone her disaray . . .

and concludes

> Now it is night, ye damsels may be gon,
> And leave my love alone,
> And leave likewise your former lay to sing:
> The woods no more shal answere, nor your echo ring.

Thus the problem of unity and integration, on which we have so far dwelled, leads us to another important aspect of the poem, its organic growth and its time-consciousness. Looking at comparable longer poems of the period we find that no consistent use is made of the passing of time. Narrative poems of the pastoral kind certainly present an action which moves forward, but we are not really made to feel the lapse of time. Spenser's *Epithalamion* appears to be composed on another principle, which we might call the principle of organic growth alternating between movement and suspense, progress and immobility, for each stanza gives us a new picture and exploits a new situation which gains life before our eyes. But in almost every stanza we are also reminded that the action has moved forward and that time is passing. The natural sequence of the hours of the day serves as a "clock-time scheme." But within this "clock-time scheme" we have the subjective time experience. Time may pass quickly or it may linger on endlessly. The varying tempo produced within each stanza by versification and diction helps to produce this feeling of passing time. There are stanzas with quick movement where several things happen at once in an almost dramatic simultaneity, and there are stanzas of a lingering mood, in which time seems to stand still. The moods of expectancy and impatience, of happiness and fulfilment are invariably expressed by references to the passing of time. Thus we have the subjective experience of slow-moving time in line 280:

> How slowly do the houres their numbers spend?
> How slowly does sad Time his feathers move?

Spenser's subtle use of time contributes to the over-all effect that something is really happening in the poem, happening at this very moment; that we ourselves are taking part in this day and are watching the progress of an actual experience. Indeed we even believe that we are among the bystanders lining the road while the procession moves forward.

But how does the poet achieve this effect of immediacy and of presence? For this is perhaps the most remarkable feature in a poem handling a classical convention, and it is, moreover, an effect we do not find in the "long poems" of the Elizabethan Age. In analyzing this effect we come upon a number of devices which again no other poet of Spenser's time has used in this subtle manner. For all descriptions of events, of situations, of persons grow out of an act of looking, watching, hearing. They are not given "objectively" but are reflected by someone who watches. This may be the poet-bridegroom himself, or the boys and maidens in the street looking at the bride as she passes by, or it may even be ourselves, the audience. For we are constantly called upon to see, to gaze, to hear, to listen (cf. 64, 129, 167, 185, 223, 372, 377).[11] Even the sun and the moon, as well as the angels, are to take part in this process.[12] Thus Spenser, the painter-poet of the eye, has endowed the figures he puts into his poem with his own gift of gazing. This immediacy and directness are further enhanced by the role assumed by the

[11] Some of the stanzas actually begin with this request as, e.g.,
>   VIII   (129) Harke how the Minstrels gin to shrill aloud
>   X   (167) Tell me ye merchants daughters did ye see
>   XIII   (223) Behold whiles she before the altar stands.

[12] E.g.
>   That even th'Angels which continually,
>   About the sacred Altare doe remaine,
>   Forget their service and about her fly,
>   Ofte peeping in her face that seemes more fayre,
>   The more they on it stare (229–33).

poet himself, which we have already compared to the role of a producer or "master of the revels." For it is the poet who directly addresses the nymphs, the bridesmaids, and all other groups which turn up in the course of the day, telling them what to do, what to look at, or what to expect. Thus we find, instead of the objective statement or the detached description, the direct address, the imperative, the question. At one point the poet even addresses his own bride, for in the midst of the ceremony in the church he asks her: "Why blush ye love to give to me your hand?" (238).

Thus a dialogic partnership is established throughout the poem. Of some stanzas we can even say that the dramatic mode is employed, for we are given little scenes with the movements, gestures, and doings of various persons or groups of people. This immediacy and directness of presentation also helps to bridge the gap between the conventions—the learned allusions on the one hand and the familiar contemporary world of Spenser's readers on the other hand. For beside the conventions deriving from the epithalamic tradition, there are spread throughout the poem a great many (in fact hundreds) of references to the Bible, to classical, medieval, and Renaissance authors.[13] Spenser has absorbed and integrated this mass of learned material from myth and legend, from the literary tradition and theology to such extraordinary degree that we scarcely become aware of this background, for it has been transformed into fresh and actual experience, it has been welded and integrated into the organic texture of the poem. As Douglas Bush has shown us, there is in many Elizabethan poems an amalgam of pagan and Christian deities, of legend and mythology together with contemporary allusion,[14] but I would suggest that there is no other longer poem of the sixteenth century in which this fusion of heterogeneous material, of disparate notions and motifs has reached the same degree of perfection, at the same time successfully increasing the poem's complexity, richness, and unity.

However, in Spenser's *Epithalamion* we do not only find the muses, graces and pagan deities like Bacchus, Hymen, Hebe, and Juno side by side with the Christian angels, the "temple gates" by the altar (204, 215), but we also find very different levels of style

    [13] See the commentary by Cortlandt van Winkle (New York, 1926).

    [14] Douglas Bush, *Mythology and the Renaissance Tradition in English Poetry* (New York, 1957).

and of expression. For the scale of Spenser's language reaches from
everyday idiom up to the most elaborate diction of Elizabethan
poetry. Compare, for example, short monosyllabic phrases like:

> For they can doo it best (258)
> And in her bed her lay (301)
> That no man may us see (320)

with lines like

> Her long loose yellow locks lyke golden wyre,
> Sprinckled with perle, and perling flowres a tweene. (154–55)

And compare again these lines with the colloquial simplicity of:

> Ah my deere love why doe ye sleepe thus long (85)

or

> Enough is it, that all the day was youres. (297)

But Spenser's vocabulary in the poem also includes archaic words,
as had already been used in *The Shepherd's Calender*, though here
they are applied with more discretion.

This wide range of his linguistic and stylistic resources allows
Spenser to express changes of mood and tempo, to achieve a transition from stylization and formality to a natural and easy manner.
Of the many examples which could illustrate this point I should
like to draw attention to some contrasting stanzas. Stanza VIII
(129 ff.) gives us the bustle and noisy activity in the street with its
"confused noyce" and the sound of all the merry music, of pipe
and tabor:

> Harke how the Minstrels gin to shrill aloud
> Their merry Musick that resounds from far,
> The pipe, the tabor, and the trembling Croud,
> That well agree withouten breach or jar.
> But most of all the Damzels doe delite,
> When they their tymbrels smyte,
> And thereunto doe daunce and carrol sweet,
> That all the sences they doe ravish quite,
> The whyles the boyes run up and downe the street,
> Crying aloud with strong confused noyce,
> As if it were one voyce.

> Hymen io Hymen, Hymen they do shout,
> That even to the heavens theyr shouting shrill
> Doth reach, and all the firmament doth fill,
> To which the people standing all about,
> As in approvance doe thereto applaud
> And loud advaunce her laud,
> And evermore they Hymen Hymen sing,
> That al the woods them answer and theyr eccho ring.

But the following stanza has quite a different pace. It solemnly announces the appearance of the bride; all stir and movement come to a halt and we are arrested by the gorgeous beauty of the poetry:

> Loe where she comes along with portly pace,
> Lyke Phoebe from her chamber of the East,
> Arysing forth to run her mighty race,
> Clad all in white, that seemes a virgin best.
> So well it her beseemes that ye would weene
> Some angell she had beene.
> Her long loose yellow locks lyke golden wyre,
> Sprinckled with perle, and perling flowres a tweene,
> Doe lyke a golden mantle her attyre,
> And being crowned with a girland greene,
> Seeme lyke some mayden Queene.
> Her modest eyes abashed to behold
> So many gazers, as on her do stare,
> Upon the lowly ground affixed are.
> Ne dare lift up her countenance too bold,
> But blush to heare her prayses sung so loud,
> So farre from being proud.
> Nathlesse doe ye still loud her prayses sing,
> That all the woods may answer and your eccho ring.

The mood of solemn gravity and intimate silence finds its place in this poem as well as the mood of jolly merriment, and both are given their appropriate stylistic expression. Thus Spenser gives us in his *Epithalamion*, on different levels, "variety within unity." In emphasizing this aspect, however, we must also consider his versification. For this most elaborate and intricate stanza of eighteen or nineteen lines which Spenser developed out of the Italian *canzone* allows for changes of rhythm and tempo. Short lines alternate with long ones and the meter is often modified and shifted. A special study would be needed to show how this flexible manipulation of meter contributes toward the effect of suspense, of slowing down and speeding up, of heightening tension. And it would also be worth while demonstrating how Spenser makes use of the rhetorical figures of assonance, anaphora, alliteration, of word-echo, of inverted word order or of certain syntactical patterns to underline or intensify the significance of particular passages. It goes without saying that these "arts of language" are given masterly treatment by a poet who had gone through years of intense poetic training. But this refined instrument of poetical expression is not in itself a product of art but merely a servant. It had to find its thematic counterpart, its adequate conception and framework, in order to exert its full power.

I have limited myself to aspects of Spenser's poetic art which combine to make up the poem's high artistic quality. I have omitted Spenser's handling and modification of the genre to which this poem belongs, the marriage poem or "epithalamium" which from antiquity onward up to Spenser undergoes considerable transformation. Such a study, which has already been carried out by other scholars,[15] would confirm the impression which our reading of the poem has so far given us: that Spenser is at the same time traditional and original, typical and personal, private and public, and that the poet has carefully preserved a great many traditional motifs out of which he has built a poem of great originality.

Inquiring into the way by which Spenser includes traditional elements of the classic marriage poem makes us even more aware of Spenser's achievement. For he succeeds in combining his personal concern and his own personal experience with the objective requirements and the "super-personal" validity of the wedding poem.

However, there is one aspect related to the poem's subject matter and purpose which I cannot omit, as it is intimately connected with what I have called the poem's uniqueness. This becomes apparent when we read the last three stanzas of the *Epithalamion*, in which Spenser gives his poem an almost metaphysical or religious

[15] See note on p. 81.

turn. Here, too, the poem includes an element that points far beyond the boundaries of the conventional "epithalamium." For the love treated previously in Renaissance poetry had as a rule not been the love between a married couple but mostly love outside marriage. But Spenser, by praising his own bride and dedicating his wedding poem to his own wife, by invoking the blessing of the "high heavens" (409 ff.) for the raising of "a large posterity," gives a new dignity to the institution of marriage. This was a new development in the history of the "epithalamium" in European literature.

The last three or four stanzas may also convey a deeper meaning to all the preceding parts of the poem. For we now realize that the sensuousness and wealth of concrete detail contained in the description of the events of the wedding day and the festivities at night are only a foreground for something else that takes place on the spiritual plane. In fact, sensuality and spirituality are combined in this poem in a unique manner.[16] Spenser gives us a wealth of sensuous impressions to please our ear and eye and to stir our imagination, but he also extends our vision from this worldly level to another plane. We are made to feel that beyond and above this earthly merriment and bustle there is a higher spiritual world. The sequence of stanzas X and XI, where the appraisal of the bride's inward beauty follows on the sensuous description of her physical beauty, is only one case in point. The reference to Spenser's use of neoplatonic concepts[17] is helpful in this connection but cannot fully account for this particular feature in the poem.

Let us sum up: our reading of Spenser's *Epithalamion* has provided us with a number of characteristics which by virtue of their specific combination contribute toward the poem's excellence. Taken individually, however, none of these characteristic features would be sufficient to produce poetry of a high order. Such poetry is born out of a happy coincidence of several factors, at a climax of a poet's artistic career which coincides with a supreme moment in his own inner experience but which also is a consummation of the lyrical potentialities of a whole period.[18] To conclude our lec-

---

[16] This aspect has been particularly stressed by Lawrence W. Hyman, "Structure and Meaning in Spenser's *Epithalamion*," *Tennessee Studies in Literature*, 3 (1958): 37–42.

[17] R. Ellrodt, *Neoplatonism in the Poetry of Spenser* (Geneva, 1960).

[18] Cf. W. L. Renwick in his comments on the poem (*Daphnaïda and other Poems* [London, 1929]).

ture let us look back over the main points we have made in order
to decide whether these points may also reveal to us something of
a more general significance. We found that Spenser's *Epithalamion*
is a "long poem" carefully planned and organized round a significant center; a poem of order and symmetry in which the
outward course of events corresponds to the process of inner experience so that the outward form has become inner form. We emphasized the poem's unity and coherence, produced by several means
and on several levels, and we stated that it was a unity in spite of
its variety. We also noted the establishing of interrelationships and
correspondences between the different parts and thematic levels of
the poem. We spoke of the "concretization" of all conventions and
motifs which helped to relate every detail to a specific, concrete
moment and event during the course of the marriage day. We discussed the assimilation and integration of mythology and learned
allusions which were enlivened and brought within the reach of the
reader's familiar experience. And we mentioned the art by which
Spenser takes up many of the traditional conventions attached to
the marriage poem but uses them in such a way that they gain
actuality and new life. We noticed the sense of time, the observance
of time and locality, and we stressed the effect of immediacy, spon-
taneity, and presence which was in part produced by a dramatic
mode of presentation, and we finally hinted at the metaphysical
and spiritual level in the poem. But the most striking quality which
emerges from most of these points is the poem's inclusiveness, its
"triumphant fusion of many different elements" as C. S. Lewis,
in discussing the *Epithalamion*, has expressed it.[19] For from whatever angle we look at this poem we are struck by this inclusiveness.
Spenser's *Epithalamion* unites the epic and the lyric mode, realism
and formalism, high seriousness and jollity, mythology and contemporary custom, objective detachment and personal concern,
sensuality and spirituality, and several other such pairs of contrasting qualities.

Thus we may conclude by saying that Spenser's *Epithalamion*,
apart from its loveliness and charm, can also disclose to us the
co-operation of some basic principles of poetic art. For terms like
order, organic structure, unity in variety, amalgamation of traditional material, observance of time and locality, immediacy and

---

[19] C. S. Lewis, *English Literature in the Sixteenth Century* (Oxford, 1954), p. 373.

directness of presentation, and especially inclusiveness, designate fundamental processes which had to be attained not only in Spenser's age but in all poetry aiming at greater complexity and higher perfection. Some of these principles can be applied with particular aptness to the poetry of the Renaissance, but others are of a universal validity. The taste of a Renaissance audience was different from ours. There are, to be sure, phrases and images in this poem which may be hard to accept for a modern reader, who may also be disturbed by the amount of stylization, by the mythological invocations, by the idealizing glorification of the poet's own bride. But these are features to be appreciated within the context and against the background of English Renaissance poetry, and they do not detract from the poem's inner consistency and its perfection as a work of art. This exemplary nature of our poem may be another justification for speaking of the uniqueness of Spenser's *Epithalamion* today.[20]

NOTE: The author is under obligation for help and advice to W. L. Renwick, Robert Birley, Hans-Jürgen Diller, and Wolfgang Weiss.

[20] For this lecture I have used some of the material contained in my German study of Spenser's poem: *Spensers Epithalamion. Zum Problem der künstlerischen Wertmaßstäbe.* Sitzungsberichte der Bayerischen Akademie der Wissenschaften, Philosophisch-Historische Klasse (München, 1964, Heft 8).

Arnold Stein

❧ GEORGE HERBERT: THE ART OF PLAINNESS

As a religious poet Herbert addresses God directly or writes with the intention of being overheard by Him. For traditional and for contemporary reasons, both religious and secular in origin, he aspires to an art of plainness that can achieve absolute sincerity. He is impatient with art but must practice patience. He distrusts rhetoric—as who does not?—but in order to speak sincerely he must master the rhetoric of sincerity.

Some of his more severe claims, assertions, and rejections lend themselves, a little too easily, to the purposes of critical definition. But we do not need to take him at his word in poems like the two sonnets which, according to Walton, were addressed to his mother, or in the pair of sonnets entitled "Love" (I and II). In these poems the contest between human and divine love is presented as if it were a moral scandal, to be treated only in terms of extreme contrasts and a single range of emotion. Everything is externalized, as if a safe imaginative distance were the only proper course. If plainness has anything to do with forthrightness and with the manner attributed to plain dealers, then we must acknowledge a kind of plainness in these poems, though they lack something in art. The case against their sincerity would have to point out that the attitude assumed by the author, and eloquently expressed, does not cost him very much. The desire to believe lends energy, vividness, sharpness, but not precision, depth, or fineness to the expression. When we speak of the rhetoric of sincerity, it is not with such poems in mind.

Let us turn to a poem which does not offer a stiff rejection but raises questions, and in a very mild and casual manner seems to present a radical solution. The poem is "A true Hymne," which begins:

> My joy, my life, my crown!
> My heart was meaning all the day,
> Somewhat it fain would say:
> And still it runneth mutt'ring up and down
> With onely this, *My joy, my life, my crown.*

Herbert then goes on to defend these words, which "may take part / Among the best in art" if they are "truly said." We may suspect that the naïvety is in part cultivated; it is plainly meant, however, and comes from a refinement of knowledge rather than a lack of knowledge. These words are symbols; they represent precious wisdom, the soul of living truth which the speaker may pronounce without possessing. It is hard to say them "truly"; the heart was "meaning" them all the day, but even the heart is uncertain— "Somewhat it fain would say," and it runs "mutt'ring up and down." The value of these words, whether in private thought or in art, depends on understanding what they mean and saying them truly.

Herbert ends the second stanza with a firm declaration:

> The finenesse which a hymne or psalme affords,
> Is, when the soul unto the lines accords.

This, though it has an admirable ring and expresses one clear concept of poetic sincerity, does not quite face the problems that have been raised. The accordance of the soul may assume that the heart has understood and that the words have been "truly said," but we are not told how these vital steps are taken, or even that they have been taken. Instead, we have been given a partial definition, which is then extended by a charming example of negative illustration— a whole stanza that shows how not to do it:

> He who craves all the minde,
> And all the soul, and strength, and time,
> If the words onely ryme,
> Justly complains, that somewhat is behinde
> To make his verse, or write a hymne in kinde.

The amused incoherence of the stanza parodies the ambitious poet who starts with high resolution and finds himself hung up, forcing rhyme, splicing syntax, and barely staggering through. After the brave opening, the only words that ring true are "Justly complains." Furthermore, the grounds have been shifted, and we have not followed up the problem of how the words are to be "truly said" or how that accordance of the soul is to be achieved.

The last stanza presents a solution that is indirectly relevant to the problems of literary expression but directly relevant to the heart seeking to address God:

> Whereas if th' heart be moved,
> Although the verse be somewhat scant,
> God doth supplie the want.
> As when th' heart sayes (sighing to be approved)
> *O, could I love!* and stops: God writeth, *Loved.*

We come to see that the writing of poetry has not been at the center of the poem after all. Instead, Herbert has used art as a metaphor to express an experience of religious life. In life, if not in art, the "somewhat scant" expression of the sincere heart may be amended and completed by God. When God writes "Loved," the desire to articulate and the desire to love are at once fulfilled. Their ends are achieved without the ordinary steps of a humanly conducted process. By authoritative acknowledgment virtual expression becomes actual.

If we look at the poem from one point of view, a miracle has taken place; but from another point of view we need recognize only an inspired compression—always possible in dialogue if the correspondent understands the intention, approves it, and fully reciprocates. We may observe, therefore, that Herbert is not simply invoking a miracle, for the ends of expression may often be realized without the full use of normal means. What we cannot do, however, is take the metaphorical analogy of writing poetry as if it were literal. Sincere feelings do not of themselves produce good poems. Herbert surely knew this as well as we do. But he must also have believed that whenever he felt a poem of his to be successful, God's hand had guided his in the composition; and if he felt a poem to be successful that feeling was the sure sense that the expression had realized its end, that God had blessed the end and given him the feeling by reflection. The humility of the man of God and the humility of the artist might both acknowledge that a fumbling, "muttering" intention had by some unexpected swiftness been clarified, and that the awkward wrongness of initial and intermediate stages had somehow been transformed into the triumphantly graceful and right. In retrospect, even the labor of composition—like some fictional by-product of the creative process—might seem to be compressed into a decisive instant of time. (Poets are notoriously inaccurate in reporting on these matters and prefer to believe that their perfect poems were "dictated": which is what we prefer to believe when the evidence to the contrary does not interfere.)

There are at least two ways, then, of looking at the issues raised by this poem. I have been emphasizing the "normal" conditions of the creative process because I am primarily interested in the poet Herbert; and because I am convinced that the religious lyric, though it must fulfill special conditions, must also, and does, answer all the questions we ask of other lyrics. From a literary standpoint the central metaphor of the poem can be interpreted as analogous to the ways in which inspiration figures in the writing of poems. Inspiration is of course the kind of concept that easily crosses a line between the secular and the sacred, and for Herbert so too does the act, or the metaphor, of writing poems. In this poem we are free to interpret the analogy, so long as we recognize that it is a metaphor and is not to be taken literally. But we must also recognize that, for Herbert, though the metaphor may apply to the writing of poetry it has been superseded, as it were, by the higher form of expression to which it refers. The wisdom descending from God crowns, not with understanding but with love, an apparently clumsy human effort to understand and express. We do not expect Herbert to be dissatisfied with the attainment of such an end simply because the means do not seem to justify it. But we do not therefore think Herbert believed that this was the way to write poems, and that the individual details of thought and expression might safely be ignored because they would leap intervening stages if only "th' heart be moved." Herbert knew better, both as poet and as man of God. That he hoped, humbly, for the eaiser path of inspiration—one does not need to be either poetic or religious to feel the attraction of that course.

But Herbert's metaphors are capable of moving in more than two directions. The central fiction of writing poetry, which may refer to the real writing of poetry and to something real in the experience of religious life, may have still a third reference. In presenting the fictional account Herbert is at the same time confessing his own unworthiness, his own desire, and intimating the authentic joy which he would feel if what he is describing should happen to him. In other words, the narrative is also a concealed prayer, composed by one of the modern masters of that difficult decorum and rhetoric by means of which one may properly address God and suggest to Him certain courses for human affairs.

And so the cultivated clumsiness of the poem, the shifting of grounds, the apparent naïvety, and what may have seemed to be a radical solution to the problems of writing poetry, when taken together are something else, or several things else. But if we are at all right about the poem it cannot be taken as a simple assertion about poetry; what seems to be assertion is ultimately part of a complex and tactful statement. Yet we cannot stop here, at the satisfying literary position. We must remember that, for Herbert, the metaphor of writing is in the poem superseded by the fulfillment of the end of expression—here a confirming act which writes and rhymes as poetry but means as metaphor. If he himself believes in the fiction of his poem, then he will find its conclusion a happier one than most of his poems provide, and toward the slower, labored uncertainties of most composition he will feel some understandable impatience.

At this point, if there were time, I should want to comment on the kind of plain style we find in "The Church-Porch," and to look at some poems in which Herbert accepts, or even flaunts, a division between truth and beauty. But these poems do not finally say anything distinctive or resonant. The gestures of sincerity by which art is used to expose art can at best make but limited points. A better and more characteristic performance is "The Forerunners." Whatever else he is saying in the poem, Herbert is also bidding a fictional farewell to poetry, to the "sweet phrases, lovely metaphors," which he has rescued from the poetic "brothels" in order to bring into the church, repentant and renewed: "My God must have my best, ev'n all I had." The excitement and affection of his address could serve as well for arrival as for departure:

"Lovely enchanting language, sugar-cane,/ Honey of roses," he exclaims, as preface to imagining the unfortunate relapse as poetry returns to its old ways. He argues against what he knows will happen, and in doing so marks both a separateness of truth and beauty and the bridge of normal relations that leads to their unity:

> Let follie speak in her own native tongue.
> True beautie dwells on high: ours is a flame
>   But borrow'd thence to light us thither.
> Beautie and beauteous words should go together.

Here Platonic solution is emphasized, rather than Platonic division. The statement is handsome and, as well as we can judge from the context and from other poems, heartfelt—a major poetic belief, but not therefore the guiding inspiration of every lyrical utterance.

"Yet if you go," he adds, meaning, when you go, as the poet prepares to settle down for a final accounting:

> Yet if you go, I passe not; take your way:
> For, *Thou art still my God*, is all that ye
> Perhaps with more embellishment can say.

And so a significant division appears, if not between truth and beauty, at least between "true beauty" and what can be said in words. That words are treated as no more than a conventionally detachable garment of style may seem a little disappointing, but Herbert does at least say "perhaps." Besides, in the context of the poem "Thou art still my God" *is* an ultimate expression, one that can be and is developed in other poems but cannot be here. Its meaning cannot be improved upon, and the man preparing to give up everything will not need anything else. The expression is complete, syntactically and otherwise, as the plain saying of "My God, my King" and "My joy, my life, my crown" are not. Nor does the poet's own attitude toward poetic language remotely resemble the stiff certitude with which he elsewhere rejects the misguided efforts of misguided poets. He is not rejecting here but parting, and with fine reluctance and such sweet sorrow.

In "The Forerunners" the act of writing poetry stands for the means, made visible and audible, of communing with God; it is a human invention motivated by a borrowed flame "to light us thither," a means of returning to the source of beauty. The house of the church, the house of poetry, and the house of life, the "best room" of which is the heart, are in the poem all reduced to an essential state. As the visible church stands truly, beautifully, but imperfectly for the invisible church, so do the "sweet phrases, lovely metaphors" express imperfectly the "True beautie" on high. In its plainness the essential expression, "Thou art still my God," will fulfill the end of expression, "And if I please him, I write fine and wittie." The essentiality of the expression, when one contemplates its meaning, by itself and in the context of the poem, would seem to be better established than the poet's assurance of writing "fine and wittie." That claim one may perhaps regard as a little assertive, markedly different from the persuasive tact with which art demonstrates the limitations of art in the argument of the poem.

The distinction is a fine one but it needs to be made. I mentioned earlier that if Herbert felt a poem to be successful he would need to believe that the expression had realized its end of pleasing God, and that God had given him his feeling by reflection. But he does not practice the art of silence or the art of discovering only the essential expression, which he can then merely "mutter." He writes poems, even when their aim is to express, or transcend, the inadequacy of poetic expression. We may perhaps regard "Thou art still my God" as a symbolic plainness, an ideal to which his poetic art of plainness may aspire, but it is not itself an expression of that art.

I think we can put matters in the right perspective by drawing a distinction between the symbolic plainness of an ultimate expression and the plainness of a complete poetic action. The latter may (and in Herbert often does) move toward a clarification that resembles the symbolic plainness. But if the poetic action is complete its conclusion will be the result of a process of expression. Though the "true beauty" of "Thou art still my God" may be traced to the compressed inner meaning the expression holds for Herbert, nevertheless that statement does appear three times in the poem, and it works both with and against other statements. In "The Flower" Herbert makes another absolute statement: "Thy word is all, if we could spell." Some of his poems are advanced spelling lessons. If "The Forerunners" were, say, a poem

like "Aaron," its process might have included some parsing of the
implicit relations between "thou" and "my," or between "art"
and "still."

Herbert is acutely aware, as poet and as Christian, of deception,
evasiveness, and inadequacy within himself—and, for these, traditional attitudes toward language and art provide useful and established symbols. Besides, many of his more assertive poems take up
positions that he does not intend to carry through uncritically. A
paradox that furnishes much of his poetic material may help explain why the single attitude is often countered within its own
poem and opposed by other poems. The "grosser world," toward
the beauty and importance of which the poet feels conflicting emotions, is, in spite of his feelings, a fixed and orderly world regulated
by the "word and art" of God. It is the "diviner world of grace"
which suddenly alters, and of which God is every day "a new
Creatour."[1]

What Herbert writes in "Superliminare" may be applied to all
instances when he engages himself to "Copie out onely" this or
that. He will admit

> Nothing but holy, pure, and cleare,
> Or that which groneth to be so.

That is a program which leaves room for and grants validity to the
hopes of individual effort, without regard to cost and efficiency.
Herbert's most important subject is the mystery of God's art with
man, a subject he confronts with patience and imagination, both
passionately involved and scrupulously detached. That God's art
with man reveals God's nature he takes for granted, and he as-
sumes that the mysteries which God has concealed in man en-
courage the study of things human as an authorized reflection of
things divine.

We may put these observations together by saying that Herbert
does not give us a single, consistent attitude toward expression,
that his art of plainness does not bear a single stamp, and that his
arguments with God are conducted with great freedom and in-
ventiveness. Whenever as critics we take a single example as our
model to copy, we become aware of statements on the other side

[1] "The Temper" (II).

and of stylistic demonstrations that force us to widen our definitions. From one point of view we may be satisfied to locate the essential Herbert in the ringing declarations of "H. Baptisme" (II): "Let me be soft and supple to thy will. . . . My soul bid nothing. . . . Childhood is health." But softness must be "tempered" and suppleness must exert itself in order to be what it is. We do not know enough when we know that the goal expressed so simply is a difficult one to achieve, and that the verbal summation stands for detailed, strenuous efforts by an individual conscious that millions of human beings have in effect said the same thing and have both failed and succeeded. Our general knowledge must also "descend to particulars," for exactness lies not in any general statement but in the clarified order which poetry may achieve when particular expressions work with and against each other. In Herbert's poetry the soul has other lessons to learn, not all of them compatible with what is here presented as the sum of wisdom. For the soul that bids nothing may hear nothing; nor is that spiritual state exempt from posing and artful presumption. Childhood is not health at all in "Mortification," but is only one of several stages in the art of dying. That art would seem to be more valuable than spiritual health itself; for the art of knowing possesses more fully whatever it desires and gains, and Herbert never deviates long from this old principle, which represents the uneasy, but enduring and fruitful, marriage of Athens and Jerusalem. Childhood generally symbolizes the will in his poems, but the education of the will is the patient task of intelligence, and Herbert, to his honor, seldom trusts for long any of the attractive substitutes for intelligence. Even that most famous conversion of "The Collar"—"Me thoughts I heard one calling, *Child!* / And I reply'd, *My Lord*"—rests on the demonstration of an argument that has ruined itself.

As for his plainness, which is not all of one kind, it is above all a rhetoric of sincerity, an art by which he may tell the truth to himself and God. The major devices are not traditional figures but psychological gestures and movements. The excesses of cheerful confidence and the defections of faith decked out as humility are given their full human voice, not as exotic monsters of thought and feeling, but as common faults "whose natures are most stealing, and beginnings uncertain," faults which are most tenacious when they are not allowed to expose themselves by speaking in their "own native tongue." Belief in the divine desire for human desire grants the human feelings an essential dignity, even in error, and encourages a vigorous freedom of expression. That freedom comes under the general laws of art, and is enlarged, not restricted, by the necessities of religious tact and discipline—as it is enlarged by realizing the complex demands of poetic form.

I propose now to offer more than a token and less than a complete demonstration of his art of plainness by drawing upon three poems: "The Temper" (I), "The Pearl," and "Death."
"The Temper" (I) begins with a declaration:

> How should I praise thee, Lord! how should my rymes
>   Gladly engrave thy love in steel,
>   If what my soul doth feel sometimes,
>   My soul might ever feel!

And ends with a declaration:

> Whether I flie with angels, fall with dust,
>   Thy hands made both, and I am there:
>   Thy power and love, my love and trust
>   Make one place ev'ry where.

The "plain intention" of the poem is to transform its initial attitude into its concluding one. Our best approach, I think, is from the lines in "Love" (II) where God is asked:

> And kindle in our hearts such true desires,
> As may consume our lusts, and make thee way.

Most of "The Temper" is devoted to the consuming of false love, but the kindling of true desire coincides with the opening lines of the poem, which speak in the high hortatory voice of love convinced that it is sincere and deserves to have its way. The "how should" and the "if" mark the fiction that represents real desire and invokes the conventions of literary and religious praise. Although the power and sweep of the language obscure the personal motive, which is not in the conventions of praise an illegitimate one, Herbert's characteristic exercise of religious propriety never allows personal desire to speak for the whole man without some discriminating process of clarification. "Gladly engrave thy love in steel" rings beautifully, but pretends to forget that the only standard is God's approval of the offering. The poet's desire is not absurd, but he knows that its expression is, and he compensates in the second stanza by acting out his pretentiousness. If there are forty heavens, or more, when things are right with him he can "peere" over them all. At other times "I hardly reach a score." And sometimes there is a general minus, without arithmetic: "to hell I fall." The kindling and consuming are most intense in the next three stanzas, which clarify the issues and stand apart from the first and last two stanzas. In these middle three stanzas the excesses of pride and humility strive against each other in images of expansion and contraction, and in the movements up and down of actual and psychological space:

> O rack me not to such a vast extent;
>> Those distances belong to thee:
> The world's too little for thy tent,
>> A grave too big for me.

> Wilt thou meet arms with man, that thou dost stretch
>> A crumme of dust from heav'n to hell?
> Will great God measure with a wretch?
>> Shall he thy stature spell?

> O let me, when thy roof my soul hath hid,
>> O let me roost and nestle there:
> Then of a sinner thou art rid,
>> And I of hope and fear.

This last stanza (the fifth) is like the first in advancing personal desire while paying tribute to God. We may note that the eloquence of humility is no less moving, no less an expression of real desire, and no less wrong, than the eloquence of pride. By now the two extremes have exhausted each other, and some *tertium quid* must be called on to make peace. The sixth stanza explains the emblematic title, declares acceptance of the divine will, and advances the metaphor of music as a solution to the problem of praise:

> Yet take thy way; for sure thy way is best:
>> Stretch or contract me, thy poore debter:

> This is but tuning of my breast,
>   To make the musick better.

And so the stanza completes the action of consuming false love by translating the experiences of the poem into terms of acceptance which draw a moral. The metaphor of music discovers a retro-active purpose in the contradictions, a purpose which may also govern present and future action. But Herbert does not stop here, for the kindling and consuming have served "to make thee way," and the seventh stanza is the demonstration of what can happen when way has been made for God:

> Whether I flie with angels, fall with dust,
>   Thy hands made both, and I am there:
> Thy power and love, my love and trust
>   Make one place ev'ry where.

One may perhaps describe the metaphor of music as a rational discovery which orders in a quiet, reasonable way the passionate contradictions which have been expressed. But the final stanza establishes, without reference to music, a concord that is more comprehensive. In the language of religion the difference resembles that between intellectual acceptance and entire resignation. Herbert himself might well have thought that the old, restrictive terms were consumed in order to make way for the new, and that he was himself, in a minor, personal way, copying the process by which truth had once come to light—in Augustine's summary statement: "the New Testament reveals what was concealed in the Old."[2] In "The Quip" Herbert refuses the arguments of his opponents for he has a single answer ready penned; here the arguments come from his own soul and he must work through them to reach his answer. The simple perfection of that answer cannot be antici-pated but comes suddenly, and after a slight pause.

Although the final stanza may be said to express and to demon-strate religious resignation, we may approach it from the traditions of rhetoric. First, we may draw on Aristotle's point that of the three "modes of persuasion furnished by the spoken word" the most important, by and large, is "the personal goodness revealed

---

[2] *City of God*, V, xviii.

by the speaker"; in fact, "his character may almost be called the most effective means of persuasion he possesses."[3] Christian rhetoric accepts the point and advances it; where the unity of eloquence and wisdom occurs we may assume the effective presence of inspiration as a proof of character. The chief goal of eloquence is to move, and Christian high style could be thought of as assimilating all the characteristics of the plain style, deriving its elevation primarily from the personal fervor with which the saving truth was expressed.

The last stanza will not fit into a rhetorical category of style. It is adorned and elevated, but the dominant effect is that of plainness and simplicity. The graces of art are subtle though not inscrutable; and we could point to devices not in the handbooks of rhetoric (as Augustine is pleased to note of a passage from the Book of Amos),[4] and perhaps not even in the annals of microlinguistics. But we may spare that demonstration for now. The issues of the poem are resolved in a final expression that unites beauty and truth, eloquence and wisdom. There is no point of leverage for distinguishing between what is said and the authoritative gift of being able to say it: inspiration is the proof of character. An expression as complete and as final in its way as "Thou art still my God" has emerged from a developing pattern of conflict; and although that expression can stand alone, it was created in the act of completing the poem, and it answers all the immediacies of conflict and form. It can stand alone but does not insist on its privilege, as a few ready-penned expressions make some show of doing. We may perhaps apply Herbert's metaphor of wisdom descending from above, the silk twist let down; though in "The Pearl" inspiration must precede and direct the poem in order to be present for the final confirmation. Or we may say that in "The Temper" when the poet stopped God wrote "loved" and spelled it out in a whole stanza.

Our next example is "The Pearl," a poem with a simpler argument and a basic plot—that of rejecting the ways of the world, the flesh, and the devil, each in a stanza. A final stanza explains why, clarifies the issues, confirms the character of the speaker, and in a simple statement organizes the procedures of the poem into their

---

[3] *Rhetoric*, I, ii (1356ᵃ).
[4] *The Christian Doctrine*, IV, vii (15–20).

completed form. We find no acting out of inspiration at the end, but instead a quietly effective definition of the ways of love and understanding. In the penultimate stanza, for the sake of an ultimate plainness the poet unexpectedly elevates the plain style that has been serving him with perfect ease and variety.

The plot is basic and the formula for human temptation is the standard one, but Herbert's conception and performance are markedly fresh and individual. The temptation of the devil, as intellectual pride, he puts first. It is not a temptation at all but little more than an inventory, and not even an explicit rejection. By putting intellectual pride first but not treating it as pride, and by his casual manner and racy diction, he exhibits a surprising and witty indifference to the traditional power of that temptation. Indeed, if we do not recognize the historical issue, the first appearance of the refrain, "Yet I love thee," may seem a little forced and overemphatic. As the poem develops, and as we collect our bearings in motion, we are supposed to recognize that pride is not being located in the intellect alone but is distributed throughout all decisions involving a choice between the love of self and the love of God. In the second stanza the temptations of the world are rejected, without the dignity of a formal recognition but in the course of drawing up an inventory of the ways of honor. The casual raciness becomes intensified, and the tone advances to open mockery:

> I know the wayes of Honour, what maintains
> The quick returns of courtesie and wit:
> In vies of favours whether partie gains,
> When glorie swells the heart, and moldeth it
> To all expressions both of hand and eye,
> Which on the world a true-love-knot may tie,
> And bear the bundle, wheresoe're it goes:
> How many drammes of spirit there must be
> To sell my life unto my friends or foes:
>   Yet I love thee.

Then the third and climactic stanza presents the temptation of the flesh, the ways of pleasure. One does not expect to meet sensitively intelligent Christians who are confident that they are untempted by intellectual pride and the subtle allurements of the world; one expects even less to learn that so rare a person is frankly responsive to the appeals of pleasure:

> I know the wayes of Pleasure, the sweet strains,
> The lullings and the relishes of it;
> The propositions of hot bloud and brains;
> What mirth and musick mean; what love and wit
> Have done these twentie hundred yeares, and more:
> I know the projects of unbridled store:
> My stuffe is flesh, not brasse; my senses live,
> And grumble oft, that they have more in me
> Then he that curbs them, being but one to five:
> > Yet I love thee

These are not, to be sure, the common temptations of the flesh but reflect a refined, more philosophical, concept of pleasure—as if Herbert were revising Socrates' fable in the *Phaedrus* and attributing rebelliousness to the spirited horse of the psychic team. A twentieth-century reader might resent the antique novelty of assigning the products of culture to the ways of pleasure, but he might find some compensation in the formal emphasis on knowledge that echoes through the stanza: "mirth and musick *mean*," and the introductory expression, "I know," is used a second time only in this stanza. What is most distinctive, however, is the passionate immediacy, the full identification of the poet with the feelings expressed. The nonchalance of witty indifference abruptly disappears; and the stanza excludes, for the moment, those quantitative images of profit and loss which partly reflect the amused detachment and superiority of the speaker—the "stock and surplus," "quick returns," "gains," and "drammes of spirit." The controls of knowledge and love are not broken down, but they remain external and neither repress the feelings nor enter into their expression. As for the temptation itself, it is not considered in a formal way, but its presence and force are amply represented by the language of the speaker.

As a measure of Herbert's boldness and candor it is useful to quote an authoritative diagnosis of the symptoms and etiology of imaginative self-temptation. When, according to Augustine, the soul slackens in its powers of determination, the body will try to advance its own interests. Delighted by "corporeal forms and movements," the soul then "becomes entangled with their images

which it has fixed in its memory, and is foully defiled by the forni-
cations of the phantasy." When the soul places the end of its own
good in the sensuous, it "snatches the deceptive images of corporeal
things from within and combines them together by empty thought,
so that nothing seems to it to be divine unless it be of such a kind
as this."[5] Augustine's diagnosis, with its adaptation of Platonic and
Stoic features, may describe the rebellious imagination as we see
it, for instance, in "The Collar," and it may help identify an occasional lapse in Herbert's spiritual nerve, but it is remarkably
irrelevant to the "corporeal forms and movements" of his third
stanza. The feelings expressed there have dignity; they are immediate and real, without defilement and resulting self-hatred, and
without confusions of the divine. In fact, only the ways of honor
come directly under Augustine's analysis, for they are the artificial
products of illusive symbolizing, the "deceptive images" patched
together with "empty thought."

The first and second stanzas, we noted, resemble each other in
their amused detachment. Their plain style is that of argument,
which demonstrates indirectly, by witty analysis, that the major
temptations do not tempt at all. The greater intensity of the second
stanza by moving toward mockery increases the imaginative distance between the objects discussed and the speaker. The plain
style of the last stanza will reverse that direction. It is argument,
and intellectual, but not detached. Everything is drawn together,
and toward the poet at the center of his experience. But the decisive change is initiated by the third stanza with its personal fervor
and elevated style.

Let us compare in their relations these last two stanzas and the
last two stanzas of "The Temper" (I). In that poem the penultimate
stanza ("Yet take thy way; for sure thy way is best") presents an
intellectual acceptance which is rather dry and detached but provides the necessary bridge to the comprehensive solution of the last
stanza, which is highly charged with feeling but registers as an
inspired clarification. In "The Pearl" the general procedure is the
same but the parts are reversed. The conflict does not take shape
until the penultimate stanza, where the climax also occurs; that

---

[5] *The Trinity*, XII, 9 (14)–10 (15), trans. Stephen McKenna (The Catholic University of America Press, 1963).

stanza brings about the shift in direction from analytical distance to synthetic immediacy, as the necessary bridge to the comprehensive solution of the last stanza. In "The Pearl" it is the penultimate stanza which is elevated in style and charged with feeling. But its expression is, though intense and candid, consciously limited by the external controls of the context; it cannot speak for the whole man in the poem. Though eloquent and moving, the voice of the stanza cannot possibly bring eloquence and wisdom into the unison of a single speech. The last stanza names inspired wisdom as a presence which has governed the whole action of the poem, but which does not, as in "The Temper" (I), make a personal appearance. The clarification of love and understanding is quietly intellectual, not passionate, and includes the humble disclaimer that whatever has been accomplished by the poem was merely by following instructions:

> Yet through these labyrinths, not my groveling wit,
> But thy silk twist let down from heav'n to me,
> Did both conduct and teach me, how by it
>   To climbe to thee.

In this poem there is no pause inviting God to write the last stanza; an affirming act of the intellect builds on a moment of passion, rather than the reverse. But the proof of character lies in the integration and in the poet's being at one with what he says. There has been no spectacular inspiration, but everything has been drawn together, and the silk twist which has led him through the labyrinths has brought him to the expressive center of what he concludes.

Our final example is the poem "Death," which acknowledges no conflict. The fictional pretext is a slight and transparent one: the difference between the way we used to look at death and the way we look at it now. The plot is not likely to surprise, and since there is no formal conflict the poet's own feelings do not directly participate in the action. Coming to the poem after "The Temper" (I) and "The Pearl," one is at first perhaps more conscious of the differences, but the similarities are more significant.

As in many poems that are relatively straightforward and simple in statement, Herbert invents fine devices on which the materials turn, move, and develop—as if they were proceeding by

means of the more visible structures of argument, dramatic conflict, or narrative plot. Each stanza of "Death" is a kind of self-
contained scene, into which the last line brings an unexpected
effect. The reader is not likely to be aware that an argument is
also being produced, until he encounters the open "Therefore" at
the beginning of the sixth and last stanza. There are three parts
of the argument, arranged in a formal diminution of 3:2:1. The
first three stanzas give us the old wrong views of death, the next
two corrected present views, and the conclusion is drawn in a
single stanza. Let us begin with the first three:

> Death, thou wast once an uncouth hideous thing,
> Nothing but bones,
> The sad effect of sadder grones:
> Thy mouth was open, but thou couldst not sing.

> For we consider'd thee as at some six
> Or ten yeares hence,
> After the losse of life and sense,
> Flesh being turn'd to dust, and bones to sticks.

> We lookt on this side of thee, shooting short;
> Where we did finde
> The shells of fledge souls left behinde,
> Dry dust, which sheds no tears, but may extort.

The mementos of death are handled with remarkable verve and
gaiety. Of "The Temper" (I) we could say that the intention of
the poem was to transform its initial declaration into its concluding
one. Here we have attitudes rather than declarations; and that
strange, bluff greeting to death, though startling, original, and
arbitrary, does not register at once as a "wrong" attitude asking
for correction. Nevertheless, the tone is the exaggerated one of an
extreme which the development of the poem will transform. If we
borrow an observation from our study of "The Pearl," we may
describe the speaker's opening attitude as detached and superior,
as if enjoying his analytical distance from the object of his attention. In the fifth stanza the tone will be countered by an opposite
extreme of immediacy and identification. Then the argument, expression, and tone of the last stanza will transform the extremes of
psychic distance and immediacy into a final attitude.

The second and third stanzas drop the concentrated focus on skull, bones, and grinning jaws, and drop the harsh, summary definition of life as a music of groans, and death as the arrested image of that music. The reason now given for that hideousness is not concentrated and shocking but leisurely and general, as befits an intellectual speculation prefaced by "For we consider'd." The error in human understanding is caused by our faulty sense of time. We think in spans of six or ten years from now and judge death by its appearances then. The detachment is quietly intellectual but does not therefore eliminate some tension of divided attitude. The reader will not find that the studied casualness of rhythm, tone, and detail prevents him from considering any thought of his own death, "some six / Or ten years hence." Furthermore, the ironic turn in the last line of each stanza reintroduces the opportunity for personal concern and relation: "Flesh being turn'd to dust, and bones to sticks. . . . Dry dust, which sheds no tears, but may extort." And that beautiful euphemism for skeletal remains, "The shells of fledge souls left behinde," is a little too successful; we admire the imaginative act and in so doing are reminded of the natural state of the material thus translated.

In addition to these psychological movements which endue a sense of developing conflict, we may note the presence of significant attitudes toward time. The first stanza greets death as it was, not once upon a time but "once," as it was in time past. But the imaginative time of that stanza is the feeling-present, which the shock of the image produces, in spite of the summary intellectualizing of the cause in the immediate past and the assertion that all of this visible effect is not what it seems to be but is what it was "once." The assertion is left dangling as a challenge that is to be made good, but not in the formal time of the second and third stanzas, which does not go all the way back to the "once." The feeling-present returns, though less emphatically, in the suggestions of personal death and in the reference to the dust "which sheds no tears, but may extort." Still more elusively, the sense of future time enters these stanzas. There is an ambiguity in the "six / Or ten years hence"—depending on whether we were considering the case of stanza one, or were considering some case, perhaps our own, from a point in the past identical with our consideration and extending six to ten years into the future. But since the point in the past is not located firmly, the sense of future time is at best weak. Similarly, the flesh and bones "being turn'd" to dust and sticks presents us with a free composition of past, present, and future; any single dimension of time can dominate in that formula, depending on the formal perspective. Finally, the "fledge souls" do evoke the future in a definite but small way; the transaction itself points ahead, and the habits of metaphorical thought on this familiar subject move naturally from the place "left behinde" to the far future.

Everything we have considered thus far will reappear, with changes, in the next step of the argument, which begins in the fourth stanza:

> But since our Saviours death did put some bloud
> Into thy face;
> Thou art grown fair and full of grace,
> Much in request, much sought for as a good.

The verve and gaiety continue, but now the mementos of death are looked at from the perspective of life after death. Out of the conventions of that perspective Herbert draws details that emphasize the imaginative nature of his presentation. The hideousness of the skull in the first stanza was the product of its appearance, our perspective, and the grotesque associations brought to bear. In the fourth stanza the perspective and associations are changed; a show of appearance is made, but the literal, physical terms are dominated by their symbolic and metaphorical meanings. The language is matter-of-fact, "But since our Saviours death did put some bloud / Into thy face," and more comforting than "Thy mouth was open, but thou couldst not sing"; but both statements are self-consciously imaginative, two opposing ways of looking at death, each an exaggeration based upon a different view of the truth. The stanza continues to emphasize its imaginative play as it moves further from the possibility of literal presentation. Both the face which is now "fair and full of grace" and the beholder's eye are altered, and the newness of the relationship is underlined by the pleasantry of "grace." The last line of the stanza draws back a little, with a kind of wry humor far gentler than the irony in each of the preceding last lines. Death is "Much in request"—as if by a change in fashion. That death is "much sought for as a good" moves the significance further from its physical base and advances the dignity of its attractiveness by the deliberate introduction language that has philosophical associations.

The "But since" which opens the fourth stanza is the sign both of argument and of time. Though the dominant time-sense is present it is derived from the Savior's act in the past and lightly suggests the future in "sought for as a good." The sense of the present, however, is not *felt* as in the first stanza but serves mostly as a kind of intellectual transition to the strong present of the fifth stanza. Finally, to touch again on the point of imaginative distance: the fourth stanza maintains a distinctive kind of detachment, because of its intellectualized emphasis on the metaphorical and the witty.

The fifth stanza completes the corrected view of death, bringing the poem to a sudden climax:

> For we do now behold thee gay and glad,
> > As at dooms-day;
> When souls shall wear their new aray,
> And all thy bones with beautie shall be clad.

Each of the first three stanzas presents a thesis abruptly at the beginning and then makes additional points to tighten and complicate the scene. In the fourth and fifth stanzas the thought requires the whole four lines for its development, and in the fifth stanza rises to a declarative climax in the last line, reversing the established ironic twist of the first three stanzas and the mildly humorous withdrawal of the fourth. More important, all of the motions of detachment, all of the varieties of analytical distance in the poem are reversed in the sudden rush of imaginative immediacy.

The developing attitudes toward time are also brought to a climax, but the details are more involved and cannot be seen without analysis. Let me summarize briefly. In the first three stanzas the formal time was past, the finished past of "once" in the first stanza and a less definite, recent past in the second and third stanzas. But in the first a sense of the feeling-present dominates; in the second and third present and future both enter, but elusively. In the fourth stanza a similar blend occurs, though the formal time is present. But when we come to the fifth stanza, suddenly there is no sense of the past. The present dominates but draws its intensity from a

prophetic vision of the future. That future comes into the poem
strongly and positively at this one point, and fully answers the
finished past of stanza one. Since that future is imagined as intensely present, the effect is a formal reply to the feeling-present
of stanza one.

These answers composed of the oppositions of time and the oppositions of psychic direction are not conclusive. A quiet "Therefore"
converts their striking emphasis into mere transition, as if the real
answer has been waiting for the commotion to subside:

> Therefore we can go die as sleep, and trust
> Half that we have
> Unto an honest faithfull grave;
> Making our pillows either down, or dust.

Now the time is wholly present: it is the unique product of imagined
past and future, but emerging also from the varying stresses on the
present which have been drawn like a thread through the labyrinth
to this open place. As for either analytical detachment from death
or imaginative identification—the final attitude rejects the terms
of the contradiction, but draws an essential indifference from detachment and an essential acceptance from identification. The
human present of the last stanza copies the calm of eternity, into
which no agitations of past or future intrude. Death is not an alien
object exciting mixed emotions, nor a lover to be sought and em-
braced. The imagination of the poem has made death familiar and
neutral; it can have no place even in dreams when it has been
made subject to a common, everyday idiom which says, "we can
go die."

The activity of the mind is less prominent than in the conclusion
of "The Pearl," but as in that poem an affirming act of the intellect
quietly builds on a moment of passion, and the mind that dismisses
itself has demonstrated the power and clarity of its self-possession.
There is no pause, as in "The Temper" (I), inviting God to write
the last stanza. The spectacular inspiration comes in the prophetic
vision of doomsday, which is followed by the rarest kind of personal
clarity, casual and laconic, as if inspiration were part of the everyday order and could be taken for granted. The final state of simplicity is not one of reduced but of alert, refined consciousness.
One sign is the attitude toward the body, which is no less than

"Half that we have." And even more remarkable than calling the grave "honest" and "faithfull" is doing so with the air of not saying anything unusual. As in "The Pearl," the excited elevation of style in the penultimate stanza is followed by an authoritative descent to the plain style. In "Death" it is an assimilative plain style, confidently challenging comparison with the height of the preceding stanza. The power of that plain style lies in the passion excluded, in the resistance mastered, and in the deliberate grace of saying difficult things with ease. The grandeur and force of the high style are achieved while talking in an off-hand, humble manner in the common imagery of going to bed. An enlightened rhetorician would observe that this plain style does not austerely reject ornament, which may persuade but must first provide esthetic pleasure. He would add, I am sure, that these graces of style are so natural and fine as to seem in the very grain. The last line, "Making our pillows either down, or dust," awakens a delicate echo of the earlier ironies, as a farewell touch of recognition. And the order of "die as sleep" is beautifully reversed and balanced by "down, or dust."

I shall end by introducing another viewpoint for a moment. In reading Donne Coleridge described the delight of "tracing the leading thought thro'out the whole," by means of which "you merge yourself in the author, you *become He.*"[6] Herbert he declares to be "a true poet, but a poet *sui generis*, the merits of whose poems will never be felt without a sympathy with the mind and character of the man." A true poet who requires a conscious act of sympathy would seem to have a different and lesser merit than the poet who compels you to "*become He.*" Coleridge justly admires Herbert's diction, "than which nothing can be more pure, manly, and un-affected." But some of the thoughts are "quaint," and he does not try to follow a leading thought throughout. Identifying oneself with the author would seem to be a modern extension of the most important mode of rhetorical persuasion, "the personal goodness revealed by the speaker" in ancient rhetoric, or the inspired unity of wisdom and eloquence in Christian rhetoric. The merits of identifying oneself with the poet are debatable. But we can draw

---

[6] These passages are collected in *Coleridge on the Seventeenth Century*, ed. R. F. Brinkley (Duke University Press, 1955), pp. 523, 534.

two firm points from Coleridge's remarks. First, it is clear that Herbert is a master who draws a leading thought through authentic obstacles which both test and refine the ultimate expression of that thought. Secondly, the rhetorical proof of character lies in the poet's convincing demonstrations that *he* becomes what he says, that the flow and shape of his words lead to a unity of eloquence and wisdom, and that he is at the expressive center of what he concludes.

It is tempting to end here, adding only that there are many true poets but few masters of this art of plainness. But it may be well to back up and remember that Herbert's art of plainness is an art and not a summary feature. If we have touched on the essential quality, good; but we can no more do without a full apparatus for understanding his art than he could write poems by plainly saying "Thou art still my God."

Roy Harvey Pearce

✣ WHITMAN AND OUR HOPE FOR POETRY

I take as an initiating text part of the second section of Robert
Duncan's "A Poem Beginning with a Line by Pindar." Here
Duncan looks back toward an aging Whitman; tries to recover a
sense of Whitman's special, if waning, authority as poet in the
Gilded Age; imagines how it was to be that Whitman, now—his
stroke-affected speech at once a literal and symbolic vehicle—
fumbling for the words with which to comprehend his society, its
politics, and its failure to find leaders it does not quite deserve.
Duncan sees the failure; and, like Whitman, he will not interpret
it as a betrayal of the poet. For Duncan sees that Whitman as poet
succeeded not as he portrayed failure, but rather as he gave us the
means to measure success, thus to know that our forebears' failures,
and our leaders', may well be our own. A society does not betray
its poets—the argument implicitly goes; rather, it betrays itself.
Its poets may indeed betray themselves—when they refuse to, or
simply cannot, bear witness to what they see. If, bearing witness,
they falter as did the aging Whitman, theirs are not failures but
rather "glorious mistake[s]." The line from Pindar with which
Duncan's poem begins is "The light foot hears you and the brightness begins." And it is the light-footed poet of our age who listens
to Whitman and sees illumined his world—and ours—in its present
condition.

This is the passage from Duncan's poem:

> . . . It is toward the old poets
> we go, to their faltering,
> their unaltering wrongness that has style,

123

their variable truth,
the old faces,
words shed like tears from
a plenitude of powers time stores.

A stroke. These little strokes. A chill.
The old man, feeble, does not recoil.
Recall. A phase so minute.
Only a part of the word in- jerrd.

The Thundermakers descend,

damerging a nuv. A nerb.
The present dented of the U
nighted stayd. States. The heavy clod?
Cloud. Invades his brain. What
if lilacs last in *this* dooryard bloomd?

Hoover, Roosevelt, Truman, Eisenhower—
where among these did the power reside
that moves the heart? What flower of the nation
bride-sweet broke to the whole rapture?
Hoover, Coolidge, Harding, Wilson
hear the factories of human misery turning out commodities.
For whom are the holy matins of the heart ringing?
Noble men in the quiet of morning hear
Indians singing the continent's violent requiem.
Harding, Wilson, Taft, Roosevelt,
idiots fumbling at the bride's door,
hear the cries of men in meaningless debt and war.
Where among these did the spirit reside
that restores the land to productive order?
McKinley, Cleveland, Harrison, Arthur,
Garfield, Hayes, Grant, Johnson,
dwell in the roots of the heart's rancor.
How sad "amid lanes and through old woods"
echoes Whitman's love for Lincoln!

There is no continuity then. Only a few
posts of the good remain. I too
that am a nation sustain the damage
where smokes of continual ravage
obscure the flame.

> It is across great scars of wrong
> I reach toward the song of kindred men
> and strike again the naked string
> old Whitman sang from. Glorious mistake!
> that cried:
>
> "The theme is creative and has vista."
> "He is the president of regulation."
>
> I see always the under side turning,
> fumes that injure the tender landscape.
> From which up break
> lilac blossoms of courage in daily act
> striving to meet a natural measure.[1]

Duncan's discovery of Whitman is like that of many of his contemporaries. I have chosen to begin with a lengthy passage from his work rather than with a florilegium of bits and pieces from poems of his contemporaries, because bits and pieces, however many of them there could be, simply will not convey the particular import of this, the newest version of our poets' continuing discovery of Whitman.

For the history of American poetry could be written as the continuing discovery and rediscovery of Whitman, an on-going affirmation of his crucial relevance to the mission of the American poet: which is, as it is everywhere, simply to tell us the truth in such a way that it will be a new truth, and in its newness will renew us and our capacity to have faith in ourselves, only then together to try to build the sort of world which will have that faith as its necessary condition. Our great modernist poets—Eliot, Stevens, Pound, Crane, and Williams—of course all registered in their poems their discovery of Whitman, a discovery made sometimes, as it were, in spite of themselves. Their Whitman, however, is not quite the Whitman of Duncan and his contemporaries—our contemporaries—as their hope for poetry is not quite that of Duncan and his, and our, contemporaries. Their Whitman was the lonely Adamic figure—in Emerson's phrase, the self against the world; the poet struggling to define his vocation in a world which seemed to have no place for him; the shape-shifter who at the end

---

[1] *The Opening of the Field* (New York, 1960), pp. 63–64.

tricked himself into believing that it was more important to be a
divine than a literatus. Their concern, one with their commitment
to define their vocation in their time, was to separate the literatus
from the divine and to learn from him all they could. They were
little interested in—indeed, were suspicious of—the poet as directly
critical of and deeply involved in society, politics, the structure and
function of American life and its sheer busyness. They were react-
ing, of course, against the quasi-deification which was Whitman's
boon at the end of his life and immediately after—and also against
the politically reductionist understanding of his work in interpretations like those of Parrington and Arvin. They wanted clarity, even
if it meant sacrificing charity. And their poems show that they
achieved it, and so often precisely at such a cost.

The situation is otherwise now—as Duncan's lines show. Duncan
sees those "lilac blossoms of courage in daily act / striving to meet
a natural measure." And he will say, with Whitman, that he too
is "a nation" which sustains "the damage / where smokes of continual ravage / obscure the flame." And, like Whitman, he is concerned with our leaders, our *political* leaders. In 1860, Whitman had
written "To a President":

> All you are doing and saying is to America dangled mirages,
> You have not learn'd of Nature—of the politics of
>   Nature you have not learn'd the great amplitude,
>   rectitude, impartiality,
> You have not seen that only such as they are for
>   these States,
> And that what is less than they must sooner or later lift off
>   from these States.[2]

Duncan, in his address to Presidents, is contemporary by virtue
of being Whitmanian. For his peers in our time are—whatever their
local affiliations—determined to put political and social criticism
back into their poetry. Clarity, yes. And often bitterness of apocalyptic depths; often barbaric howls over the rooftops of our world;
often a deliberate and vulgar courting of confusion; often a seeking
of shortcuts to poetic insight, which manifest themselves as short-

---

[2] Here and in what follows I quote the poems, except when noted, from *Leaves of Grass*, Comprehensive Reader's Edition, ed. H. W. Blodgett and Scully Bradley (New York, 1965).

circuits in communication. But still at the end: charity. Such charity demands an unflinching attempt at scope and inclusiveness, and so urges our poets to see the poet involved in the whole of his world, to claim—often tendentiously—that a condition of the whole poet is a commitment to understand the whole world. Duncan of course knows the work of Pound and Williams well; he has gone to school to Charles Olson, and he is immensely learned— a poet-scholar. Still, on behalf of the poets of our age, he evokes Whitman as he would seek the spirit "that restores the land to productive order." This is, in our time, our poets' hope for poetry. And they would make it ours.

My task thus is to be exegete and advocate of that Whitman who sought the spirit "that restores the land to productive order." There are other Whitmans, I remind you, and valid ones. But this is the one whom we appear to need now. I must accordingly turn to an old problem in Whitman criticism: that of the poet as critic of society. And I shall hope to show that the Whitman Duncan has recently discovered is one of the Whitmans American scholar-critics have also recently discovered. At the very least, the one discovery—by the poet—illumines the other—by the scholar-critics—and vice-versa. I should like to think that each entails the other. That is one of my hopes for poetry.

The difficult fact is that we know almost too much about Whitman as critic of American society, pre- and post-Civil War. Inevitably, those who interpret Whitman must write about his "social thought"—inevitably, because it is an integral aspect of his life's work that he should have been a "social critic." In this role he is regularly present in histories of American thought— social, political, and otherwise. This is only proper. For with great and glorious ease and freedom, the newspaperman become poet tells us in the Preface to the 1855 *Leaves of Grass* that as poet he is nothing if not critic of society. He will make his society know all its possibilities and how it may realize them.

Now, the way to that realization is, in the poems of the 1855 *Leaves of Grass*, not so much social as individual, as we all by now surely know. And the tendency of that recent strong line of interpreters of Whitman which prefers the 1855 version of his book to all others is, in fact, to deny him, as poet, much of a role as social critic—or at best to deny him a covert role. Yet even this line of interpreters sees the journalistic work which surrounds the 1855 *Leaves of Grass* as genetically related to it. That is to say, as journalist, Whitman came to know his world in closely examined and expressed detail; and consequently as poet he came to see that what his world needed was a new, or renewed, image of man, whereby it might at long last realize its potentialities. The poet offers himself to his society, offers himself as archetypal for all selves, and thereby rests assured that it will henceforth be whole. The genetic line is from Whitman's journalistic social criticism to his earliest important poems. Out of the world described in the journalism the poet was precipitated. Or rather, out of that world that poet precipitated himself, and in what came be to called "Song of Myself" with loving and daring precision described the act of precipitation, which was in fact an act of self-creation.

But the genesis did not stop there. For now the *poet*, by virtue of being a poet, surely had to continue to be a kind of social critic. True enough, he was no longer particularly a critic of issues and events—except when he wrote something other than poetry, which of course he continued to do. As poet, he had to find a way of speaking about his world and the facts of its life—a way which would let him be a critic by virtue of being a poet. The facts of which he came to speak were not quite those of which he could treat in his journalism, or even in his programmatic prefaces. No longer free soil, abolition, political compromises, forms of manifest destiny, and the like. Indeed, as his recent interpreters have uniformly noted, especially after the Civil War crisis, Whitman, even in his prose writing, was much less interested in specifically sociopolitical issues than he had been before. They have, as a consequence, tended to judge him as a social critic only in contexts outside his poetry, even when they have tried to interpret his post-Civil War poetry as somehow tending to pull (or push) him toward a definite political stance—ranging from that of utopian socialist to anti-ideological conservative. At this point, I must demur. For I think that Whitman, after the Civil War and into the Gilded Age, yet tried, as poet, to be social critic, and succeeded; and that the sort of social criticism he got into his poems was, when, occasionally, it worked as poetry, all the more powerful because it was not so much *pro-* or *anti-*political as *pre-*political.

I want to inquire a little into Whitman's attempt to find a means
of dealing in his poetry with the *products* of the sort of world about
which he had written at length in his journalistic prose. What—
again to echo Robert Duncan— . . . What were the conditions
which would have to obtain if the land were to be restored to productive order? For one of Whitman's great insights as poet—an
insight which makes him so truly the poet of whom Duncan
writes— . . . one of his great insights is that the world of post-
Jacksonian democracy, of the common man, of the Gilded Age,
was for good and for bad, one in which, through its increasingly
rationalized social and political and economic structure, producers
were increasingly bowed down under the weight of their products.
Whitman not only generalized, as had Emerson, that "Things are
in the saddle,/ And ride mankind." He *observed* the "things" as
they were at once bound to mankind and also bound it. And in
his post-Civil War poetry—or in some of it—he not only declared
his insight but gave his readers a means of weighing its significance
for them precisely as they would find themselves bowed down
under the weight of their products, or their society's. Whitman was
only fitfully successful in this vein; and toward the end, so I think
the poems show, the burden of his insight was too great for him.
He faltered. Yet it is not his failure which I would like to emphasize, but his success, however small: his "glorious failure"—to
quote Duncan again. It is, I think, a success story which we have
not yet read clearly, and one which, so the work of our poets now
indicates, has increasingly great significance for us.

Let me begin with the basic facts of the case: The 1855, 1856,
and 1860 versions of *Leaves of Grass* are stages in the development
of an essentially autobiographical poem. In this poem, or in these
versions of it, the poet discovers first himself, then society, then
again himself. The 1860 *Leaves of Grass* is Whitman's attempt to
write a totally humanistic poem; in it even the cycle of love and
death is contained in the magnificently autobiographical humanism which it projects. The Civil War put this humanism into
doubt, manifesting to Whitman not only anti-humanism (which
he had successfully contained in the 1860 *Leaves of Grass*) but dehumanization. The Civil War poems show the poet's sense of the
razor-edge balance between humanism and dehumanization; and
he survives, when he does, only by appealing to suprahuman
forces, as so memorably in "When Lilacs Last in the Dooryard

Bloomed." The war, then, was for Whitman a new kind of extreme situation—unlike the terrors and torments confronted in the 1855, 1856, and 1860 *Leaves of Grass*, one outside of himself, a product of forces he could in no way imagine himself or any man as containing and controlling. The technique of the pre-Civil War poems had been that of total empathy and total sympathy: give, sympathize, control. And the events of the war, like the social and personal catastrophes it produced, simply were beyond Whitman's, or any man's, powers of poetic empathy and sympathy. One could give and sympathize—as is shown by Whitman's prose memoranda on his hospital journeys and his letters to the soldiers he so lovingly tended. But one could not control. The poet was called upon to enlarge his technique, to amplify his capacities, to examine anew his role as poet. He was faced, crucially, with the discovery that a society, a community, is greater than the sum of its individual parts; that the sum somehow generates actions and events and things which may destroy the parts. The poet, in short, was now called upon to deal with the sum, whereas before he had dealt only with the parts (and with himself as the greatest part, as he had said).

"Long, too long, O land," Whitman wrote in 1865—later changing "O land" to "America"—

> Long, too long, O land,
> Traveling roads all even and peaceful you learn'd
>   from joys and prosperity only,
> But now, ah now, to learn from crises of anguish,
>   advancing, grappling with direst fate and
>   recoiling not.
> And now to conceive and show to the world what your
>   children en-masse really are,
> (For who except myself has yet conceiv'd what your children
>   en-masse really are?)

It was an enlargement of his conception of the poet which Whitman quite carefully announced in the first of the "Inscriptions" which open the 1871 version of *Leaves of Grass:*

> One's-Self I sing, a simple separate person,
> Yet utter the word Democratic, the word En-Masse.
> Of Physiology from top to toe I sing,

Not physiognomy alone nor brain alone is worthy for the
  Muse, I say the Form complete is worthier far.
The Female equally with the Male I sing.

Of Life immense in passion, pulse, and power,
Cheerful, for freest action form'd under the laws divine,
The Modern Man I sing.

The poem puts precisely Whitman's attempt to conceive anew of
his capacities as poet—here, as if by *fiat*. Note the burden of meaning which is carried by the "Yet" of the second line:

One's-self I sing, a simple separate person,
Yet utter the word Democratic, the word En-Masse.

Not the co-ordinating "and" nor the subordinating "but." Rather
the concessive "yet": which is to say, to claim, that even as the
poet celebrates himself as an archetypal ego for us all, he celebrates
us (including himself) as we (with him) compose a group. The one
celebration is claimed to be precisely the same as the other. So it
follows a few lines later that we are to have "freest action form'd
under the laws divine." Individual freedom is one with the law
which governs the group, the mass, to which the individual belongs. This is but an extrapolation of the heroically confident doctrine of the 1855, 1856, and 1860 versions of *Leaves of Grass*, of
course. But at this point in Whitman's career—as in the career of
his society—it becomes an issue which must be boldly, bluntly, and
at the outset, proclaimed. If he protests too much, we must at least
be grateful that he has the courage to protest.

The argument of this little poem is repeated in others of the
"Inscriptions" series: in "In Cabin'd Ships at Sea," "Eidolons,"
and in "For Him I Sing," for example. And the confidence it expresses is manifest in a significant number of poems published in
1871 and beyond—in the Gilded Age. I shall want later to look
at one of those poems, and see in somewhat formal terms just how
Whitman strives to enlarge his capacity as poet, so to treat of the
word democratic, the word En-Masse, by virtue of treating of the
simple separate person; how he conceives of freedom under law;
how he would celebrate the group's product in such a way as to
teach its producers how to relate it to themselves; how, in short,
as poet he is critic of society.

But first let me remind you of some of the consequences of this expanded conception of poetry for Whitman's conception of the poet. The major text here is *Democratic Vistas* (1871), which derives in good part from slightly earlier prose writing. A few quotations will serve our purpose:

> View'd, to-day, from a point of view sufficiently overarching, the problem of humanity all over the civilized world is social and religious, and is to be finally met and treated by literature. The priest departs, the divine literatus comes.

> It may be argued that our republic is, in performance, really enacting to-day the grandest arts, poems, &c. by beating up the wilderness into fertile farms, and in her railroads, ships, machinery, &c. And it may be ask'd, Are these not better, indeed, for America, than any utterances even of greatest rapsode, artist, or literatus?

> I say that our New World democracy, however great a success in up-lifting the masses out of their sloughs, in materialistic development, products, [note that word: *products*] and in a certain highly developed superficial popular intellectuality, is, so far, an almost complete failure in its social aspects, and in really grand religious, moral, literary, and esthetic results.

> [After detailing the objects and events and excitements of Brooklyn and New York]: But sternly discarding, shutting our eyes to the glow and grandeur of the general superficial effect, coming down to what is of the only real importance, Personalities, and examining minutely, we question, we ask, Are there, indeed, *men* here worthy the name?

> For to democracy, the leveler, the unyielding principle of the average, is surely join'd another principle, equally unyielding, closely tracking the first, indispensable to it, opposite . . . and whose existence, con-fronting and ever modifying the other, often clashing, paradoxical, yet neither of highest avail without the other, plainly supplies to these grand cosmic politics of ours, and to the launch'd forth mortal dangers of republicanism, to-day or any day, the counterpart and offset whereby Nature restrains the deadly original relentlessness of all her first-class laws. This second principle is individuality, the pride and centripetal isolation of a human being in himself—identity—personalism.

> The word of the modern . . . is the word Culture.
> We find ourselves abruptly in close quarters with the enemy. This word Culture, or what it has come to represent, involves, by contrast, our whole theme, and has been, indeed, the spur, urging us to engage-

ment. Certain questions arise. As now taught, accepted and carried out, are not the processes of culture rapidly creating a class of supercilious infidels, who believe in nothing? Shall a man lose himself in countless masses of adjustments, and be so shaped with reference to this, that, and the other, that the simply good and healthy and brave parts of him are reduced and clipp'd away, like the bordering of box in a garden. You can cultivate corn and roses and orchards—but who shall cultivate the mountain peaks, the ocean, and the tumbling gorgeousness of the clouds? Lastly—is the readily-given reply that culture only seeks to help, systematize, and put in attitude, the elements of fertility and power, a conclusive reply?

I should demand a programme of culture, drawn out, not for a single class alone, or for the parlors of lecture-rooms, but with an eye to practical life, the west, the working-men, the facts of farms and jack-planes and engineers, and of the broad range of the women also of the middle and working strata, and with reference to the perfect equality of women, and of a grand and powerful motherhood. I should demand of this programme or theory a scope generous enough to include the widest human area.

In short, and to sum up, America, betaking herself to formative action (and it is about time for more solid achievement, and less windy promise,) must, for her purposes, cease to recognize a theory of character grown of feudal aristocracies, or form'd by merely literary standards, or from any ultramarine, full-dress formulas of culture, polish, caste, &c., and must sternly promulgate her own new standard, yet old enough, and accepting the old, the perennial elements, and combining them into groups, unities, appropriate to the modern, the democratic, the west, and to the practical occasions and needs of our own cities, and of the agricultural regions.[3]

Thus Whitman in the process of enlarging his sense of himself as critic of society. Central to the enlarging is the introduction of the word "culture" as subsuming and interrelating art, religion, politics, family, trade—all American institutions—as "products": products which, as they are produced, at once make possible the good life in society and yet, because they transcend the individual, threaten that life. If we can trust the standard Whitman concordance, the word—and the concept—"culture" comes first into Whitman's vocabulary in *Democratic Vistas*. Where he got the word we do not know. We do know that it was much on his mind in

---

[3] *Collected Writings: Prose Works*, ed. F. Stovall (New York, 1964), II, 365–403.

the years around 1870. He planned, apparently, to write an essay
called "The Theory of Culture." In the Feinberg collection of
Whitman manuscripts there are his notes for that essay. With
Mr. Feinberg's permission, I quote what I take to be the most
important of them:

> The theory of culture fits the specialities of scholars & the literary
> class; Personalism is for universal use of living men in the practical
> world, with its qualities, fibre, storms, mixture of good & evil. The
> latter of the two has heights & flashes to which the former can never
> attain. The latter is for the Soul, the other for the Intellect. . . .

In short, Whitman was concerned to put "culture" to the test of
"personalism," so to distinguish what has in our time been called
authentic from inauthentic culture, that which enables and that
which disables the American as he seeks to live the life of the
simple, separate person, yet democratic, en masse. To discriminate
between authentic and inauthentic culture, to write poems which
would be the instrument of discrimination—this was the task of
the divine literatus. Such discrimination would be a necessary condition of the discovery, or recovery, of that of which Robert Duncan writes: "the spirit . . ./ that restores the land to productive
order."

Whitman strove to write poems of this order before the period
of *Democratic Vistas*, of course. I think of parts of "A Song of Joys,"
"Starting from Paumanok," and "As I Walk These Broad Majestic
Days"—all of which come into the 1860 version of *Leaves of Grass*,
all of which mark Whitman's awareness of the tension between the
claims of his radical humanism (that is, his "personalism") and the
claims of his burgeoning world (that is, its "culture"). And there is
"Years of the Modern," put first into the 1865 *Leaves of Grass*.
Still, the tension is somewhat slack in these poems, as the claims
and counterclaims seem naturally and easily to resolve themselves.

The tension is as tight as Whitman could allow it to be in a poem
first published in the 1871 *Leaves of Grass*, the poem which became
"Song of the Exposition." Under its original title, which is its first
line as I quote it, Whitman recited it at the opening of the Fortieth
Annual Exhibition of the American Institute, in New York, Sep-
tember 7, 1871. Retitled and somewhat changed, it went into the
1876 *Leaves of Grass* in part prefaced thus, the language recalling

that of *Democratic Vistas*. The preface enunciates the hope of Institute:

> Struggling steadily to the front, not only in the spirit of Opinion, Government, and the like, but, in due time, in the Artistic also, we see actual operative LABOR and LABORERS, with Machinery, Inventions, Farms, Products, &c., pressing to place our time, over the whole civilized world. Holding these by the hand, we see, or hope to see, THE MUSE (radiating, representing, under its various expressions, as in every age and land, the healthiest, most heroic Humanity, common to all, fusing all) entering the demesnes of the New World, as twin and sister of our Democracy—at any rate we will so invite Her, here and now—to permanently infuse in daily toils, and be infused by them.
>
> .   .   .   .
>
> Ostensibly to inaugurate an Exposition of this kind—still more to outline the establishment of a great *permanent* Cluster-Palace of Industry from an imaginative and Democratic point of view—was the design of the following poem. . . .

"Holding these by the hand. . . .": The phrase, as does so much of Whitman's self-indulgent prose, makes us wince. It is important, nonetheless; for it is yet another attempt of the poet to indicate how, as social critic, he might envisage the things, the products, of his world as at once of the simple, separate person and of the mass. This is his "programme of culture," and it entails no less than the humanization of the actually or potentially dehumanized, the products and institutions of an industrial society moving even in the 1870's precipitously toward over-development.

The poem, in its 1871 version, begins:

After all not to create only, or found only,
But to bring perhaps from afar what is already founded,
To give it our own identity, average, limitless, free,
To fill the gross the torpid bulk with vital religious fire,
Not to repel or destroy so much as to accept, fuse, rehabilitate,
To obey as well as command, to follow more than to lead,
There also are the lessons of our New World.
While how little the New after all, how much the Old, Old World![4]

Then, following immediately upon this call to give identity and freedom to all that which bulks large in the world, there is a small

---

[4] I quote the poem from the pamphlet, *After All, Not to Create Only* (Boston, 1871).

lyric intrusion, a recollection of the primal power celebrated from
the beginning in *Leaves of Grass:*

> Long and long has the grass been growing,
> Long and long has the rain been falling,
> Long has the globe been rolling round.

The body of the poem consists of Whitman's attempt to indicate
just how that primal power may be discovered in what he had
called in *Democratic Vistas* "culture"—culture in its largest, quite
modern, extended sense. He asks at length that the Muse come to
America from the Old World and find her place here. He sees her

> Making directly for this rendezvous, vigorously clearing
>   a path for herself, striding through the confusion,
> By thud of machinery and shrill steam-whistle undismay'd.
> Bluff'd not a bit by drain-pipe, gasometers, artificial fertilizers,
> Smiling and pleas'd with palpable intent to stay,
> She's here, install'd amid the kitchen ware!

Once in the New World, the Muse finds herself at home in a land
where

> We plan even now to raise, . . .
> Thy great cathedral sacred industry, no tomb,
> A keep for life for practical invention.

But how does Whitman conceive that the products of "practical
invention" may be those of authentic as opposed to inauthentic
culture? The answer is one the reader of earlier versions of *Leaves
of Grass* would expect: by seeing precisely, by expressing precisely,
the degree to which these are specifically human products; products of the simple, separate person as he is caught up in the communal life of the mass; if not the poet's own creations, nonetheless
genuine creations as they are communal creations:

> Here shall you trace in flowing operation,
> In every state of practical, busy movement, the rills of
>   civilization,
> Materials here under your eye shall change their shape
>   as if by magic,

> The cotton shall be pick'd almost in every field,
> Shall be dried, clean'd, ginn'd, baled, spun into thread and
>   cloth before you,
> You shall see hands at work at all the old processes and
>   all the new ones,
> You shall see the various grains and how flour is made and
>   then baked by the bakers,
> You shall see the crude ores of California and Nevada
>   passing on and on till they become bullion,
> You shall watch how the printer sets type, and learn what
>   a composing stick is,
> You shall mark in amazement the Hoe press whirling its
>   cylinders, shedding the printed leaves steady and fast,
> The photograph, model, watch, pin, nail, shall be created
>   before you.

The technique and the form here are familiar to us: the loving catalogue; the careful singling out of the specifically human act involved in industrial production; a dependence upon particularized nouns and verbs of human agency; an essential vitalism. I suggest that in these lines—certainly not among Whitman's greatest, but cumulating toward a certain kind of power—we know again what the poet James Wright has recently called Whitman's "delicacy." It *is* a delicacy, the total delicacy, of the human, of a poet who would (as Whitman says a few lines later) "exalt the present and the real." And he would do so by conceiving of the artisan as artist. The literatus can and must do this. So that, passing in review the very things which, produced en masse, might threaten the simple separate existence of the producers, he can in his art inquire as to the degree that they are and are not integral in the authentic existence of the producers. And at the end he can address the Muse—not God, but the Muse—simply and straightforwardly:

> Our farms, inventions, crops, we own in thee! cities
>   and States in thee!
> Our freedom all in thee! our very lives in thee!

The specific mode of this poem is one with a few others out of Whitman's later career—"Song of the Redwood Tree" (1874) and "To a Locomotive in Winter" (1876), for example. And it has

affiliations with the mode of "Passage to India" (1871). Moreover, it is a mode which we know well in Whitman's earlier
poetry—particularly in the last segment of "Song of Myself." The
difference between the mode in the post- as against the pre-Civil
War poems is this: that in the earlier poems (not only "Song of
Myself," but poems like "Salut au Monde" and "Crossing Brook-
lyn Ferry"), the poet reads himself *into* his world, whereas in the
later poems he reads an enlarged sense of other men, of humanity,
out of his world. The aim in the earlier poems was to discover himself; that of the later poems, to discover others. The later task was
the more difficult, and was performed with significantly less success, because there the poet had wherever possible to point toward
the possibility of the reassociation of that which had been, or was
in danger of being, disassociated: producer from product, actor
from act, agent from deed. He had to find a source of what he
called (in "A Backward Glance O'er Travell'd Roads,") that
"ultimate vivification" which would endow "facts," "science,"
and "common lives," "with the glows and glories and final illus-
triousness which belong to every real thing, and to real things
only." He had, in short, to locate them in social and communal
reality, to find in them at once a source and an end of culture.

"The chief trait of any given poet," he wrote in the same essay,
"is always the spirit he brings to the observation of humanity and
nature—the mood out of which he contemplates his subjects. What
kind of temper and what amount of faith report these things?"
Whitman's humanist temper and faith—for that is what the aspect
of his spirit I have been discussing comes to—only falteringly sus-
tained him after the Civil War. It would not sustain him throughout the history of "Song of the Exposition." For the 1881 version
of that poem, he added at the beginning a stanza unhappily out of
phase with what adamantly follows it:

> (Ah little recks the laborer,
> How near his work is holding him to God.
> The loving Laborer through space and time.)

The stanza is in parentheses (as an afterthought) and is meant, I
suppose, to divinize the all-too-human Muse whom the poet would
bring from abroad to dwell among the kitchenware. Only as God

could the Muse find safe-conduct in the New World. The literatus would become more divine than literate—as in so much of Whitman's later verse, with its passages to everywhere except home, the only place where the poet could honestly confront the problem of the simple, separate person and its productions en masse. But, with other scholar-critics, I have regretted this change of phase before. I regretted it, I regret it, because it diminishes Whitman's power, and his significance, for us.

And here I would dwell undiminishingly on that power and that significance. I suggest—as a way of thinking about the poet as critic of post-Civil War society—that in his own way, according to his own style, he was discovering what Marx called alienation, the alienation of the laborer from the product of his labor, in that mass-industrial society in which all men willy-nilly become laborers. The "realization of labor," so go Marx's famous words of the 1840's, "appears as *loss of reality* for the workers; objectification as *loss of the object* and *object-bondage; appropriation as *estrangement, alienation.*"

And with my quotation from Marx I return to our own time, and to the text from Robert Duncan, with which I initiated this inquiry. Let me modify two of Duncan's lines:

> Where among *us does* the spirit reside
> That restores the land to productive order?

"Productive order" is precisely the opposite of Marx's "appropriation as *estrangement, alienation.*" And "alienation" is a word which is perhaps too much with us these days. In any case, it is a word—and a concept—central to that which is most fruitful and promising in radical political thinking in our time. And, in point of fact, poets like Duncan and his peers all over our land share with all of us the discovery of "alienation" and all it implies for the fate of our culture. As I have said, they are putting politics back into our poetry. But it is a politics shot through with their sense of the matter of authentic as against inauthentic culture. They show that in an alienated world, proper politics is impossible, because cut off from the human values and capacities from which derives the very power it must organize. For them, as recent events have shown, free speech and free verse are of a piece. Accordingly, the Whitman to whom they look—although not often with Duncan's superb (and scholarly) awareness of what he is doing—is that Whitman whom I have been discussing.

Let it be freely admitted that this Whitman is, as poet, far from the greatest Whitman. "Song of the Exposition" is, as I have said, not one of the poems which stick with us; nor are the other poems in its vein, including "Passage to India." In all of them a certain religiosity and self-indulgence dull and diffuse, as if Whitman could not bear to carry out the task he set for himself. He faltered. Together, nonetheless, these poems matter deeply to us—if only in falling short of their goal, they help us all the more clearly establish our own. They show, perhaps, that Whitman was successful as prophet inversely as he was successful as poet. Together, perhaps, they amount to that "glorious mistake" over which Duncan exclaims. In all honesty, acknowledging the mistake may well be the price we must pay for apprehending the glory. And it might be possible—if we are lucky—that our poets, apprehending the glory, will not make the mistake. As ever, that must be their—and thus our—hope for poetry.

Whitman knew this well. We should recall that one of the key inscriptive poems to *Leaves of Grass* reads thus:

Poets to come! orators, singers, musicians to come!
Not to-day is to justify me and answer what I am for,
But you, a new brood, native, athletic, continental, greater
    than before known,
Arouse! for you must justify me.

I myself but write one or two indicative words for the future,
I but advance a moment only to wheel and hurry back in the darkness

I am a man who, sauntering along without fully stopping, turns
    a casual look upon you and then averts his face,
Leaving it to you to prove and define it,
Expecting the main things from you.

I add: We yet expect the main things from our poets—our poets to come—as did Whitman. Our hope for poetry now lies precisely in its search for the spirit which will restore the land to productive order.

INDEX OF AUTHORS AND EDITORS

Designed by Arlene J. Sheer

*Composed in Baskerville and Baskerville display
types by Monotype Composition Company*

*Printed offset by Universal Lithographers, Inc.
on Perkins and Squier RRR 60 lb.*

Bound by L. H. Jenkins, Inc., in Columbia Bayside Chambray